6/98

Merla —

Now don't yell. Just think
about this book – what better
way to pass the time driving
thru Texas than trying to identify
what "thing" it is on your wind-
when you get home – while you're at it
a book. Have a great trip and
Thinking of you all the
Especially thru TEXAS! H-O-T! No A/C!
Oh, My God!

Love Mom, Dad, too

P.S. What a year
to remember, Roger!

That Gunk On Your Car

THAT GUNK
ON
YOUR CAR

A UNIQUE GUIDE TO
INSECTS OF NORTH AMERICA

By Mark E. Hostetler, Ph.D.

1⊜
Ten Speed Press
Berkeley, California

Ten Speed Press
P. O. Box 7123
Berkeley, CA 94707

Library of Congress Cataloging-in-Publication Data
Hostetler, Mark.
    That gunk on your car : a unique guide to insects of North America
    / by Mark Hostetler.
       p.   cm.
    Includes bibliographical references and index.
    ISBN 0-89815-961-X
  1. Insects—North America. 2. Insects—North America
—Identification. 3. Roadside animals—North America. 4. Roadkills
—North America—Identification. 5. Insects—Study and teaching
—Activity programs—North America. I. Title.
  QL473.H67 1997
  595.7'097—dc21   97-18864
                                                              CIP

Cover design by Cale Burr
Text design by Victor Ichioka
Illustrations copyright © 1996 by Rebekah McClean
Cartoon bug graphics copyright © 1996 by Meryl Klein
Original design by Meryl Klein

Printed in Canada
1 2 3 4 5 / 01 00 99 98 97

TABLE OF CONTENTS

ACKNOWLEDGMENTS

Things have a weird way of working out: I remember the idea for this book came to me in the fall of 1991. At the time, I was working on my master's, and decided to pursue this project during the summer, after I finished most of my research. I talked about the idea with my friends, and although many of them thought I was "out there," they all encouraged me to pursue this dream I had. First and foremost is my good friend Meryl Klein, who spurred me on and was the eternal optimist. Being a novice, I had a long and frustrating experience trying to break into the publishing arena. During the four-year process, Meryl was always there to encourage me, especially when I was thoroughly frustrated and pessimistic. Further, her truly creative mind and her talent in graphics, editing, and design really put the finishing touches on this book. Her friendship and guidance were invaluable; I really appreciate working with her. Thanks, Meryl.

I am greatly thankful to Rebekah McClean (an aspiring bio-illustrator) for plopping down in my office and asking me if there were any drawing projects she could do for some experience. This was very fortunate for me, because I was in a quandary about how these insects would be drawn. I was amazed by her enthusiasm when I suggested she draw some insects and their splats. Rebekah was very patient and adaptive in interpreting exactly what I envisioned they should look like. She is just an amazing illustrator (as these drawings attest), and will surely succeed in all her endeavors.

I would also like to thank the Greyhound bus attendants from around the U.S. (especially the one in Gainesville, Florida) for allowing this strange graduate student to pick the smashed insects off the front of the buses that arrived in the depots. Further, I am grateful for the various entomologists at the Division of Plant Industry (Gainesville) that helped me identify the somewhat "altered" insects I collected. Everyone was very cooperative.

My mother, father, and brother provided me with much support and encouragement, so I could see this project to the end. Their comments and suggestions on the many drafts I produced were invaluable.

I also thank Grandma Shepherd for her understanding and monetary support to get this project off the ground. Special acknowledgment goes to Grandpa Shepherd, an entomologist and a teacher, whose interest in insects and biology inspired me to become a biologist at an early age.

Special thanks go to Leslie Klein for "power editing" the original book, and to David Dubois of Graphic Connection for his technical advice on how to get this book printed. Also, I'd like to thank the Zoology Department at the University of Florida for providing the resources necessary to help me develop into a mature student and teacher. Interactions that I have had with graduate students, faculty, and staff helped me formulate a number of the ideas included in this book. Finally, I am thankful for Kathryn Bear, an understanding editor who helped put together a terrific book in a relatively short period of time. Also, thanks goes to the many people at Ten Speed Press who worked on this project. What a terrific team!

This book is dedicated to the memory of
Grandpa C. J. Shepherd.

PREFACE

Whap! "What the heck was that? Gross! I'll have to clean the windshield; the wipers are just smearing it everywhere." Sound familiar? You have just had a close encounter with one of the many species of insects in North America. Every day thousands upon thousands of people have this experience while driving their automobiles up and down the highways of North America.

But who are these unfortunate insects? When they're not running into cars, insects lead amazingly unique and distinctive lives. Having been around for over 350 million years, insects represent greater than half of the known species of animals, and they dwell in nearly every terrestrial and aquatic habitat. Currently, close to one million insect species have been described; however, as many as three million may inhabit the Earth. The number of insects is thought to be close to 1.0×10^{18}, or approximately one billion insects for each human being. Wow! No wonder we normally encounter insects every day of our lives. Hardly a day goes by when we don't hear them buzzing around our heads, see them crawling across our paths, or feel them biting various parts of our bodies.

Even in the protective capsules of our automobiles, we cannot help but notice insects crazily careening off the front of our windshields. It's tough to get what's left of those critters off our cars! Drivers know the consequences of leaving these carcasses on their cars for an extended length of time—the paint is eventually eaten away. Industrial products to remove this gunk from your car are a million-dollar-a-year industry. Are insects just plain stupid, or were they specifically designed to degrade the beauty of our most beloved autos?

Hold on! Let's step back for a moment and take the viewpoint of the insect. For millions and millions of years, insects have been reproducing, foraging, and doing the things insects do without the influence of humans and their devices. Suddenly, about a hundred years ago, insects (as well as other animals) started having to deal with a predator that they had never encountered before—a huge hunk of metal that can go faster than forty miles per hour: the automobile. Paved roads were built for these predators (who, by the way, do not eat their prey), and now they're practically everywhere. In the past, insects have only had to worry about natural predators, such as bats, birds, and lizards, never something as big and fast as a truck. Can you imagine an insect able to detect a car in time to get out of the way?

In the search for food, shelter, and mates, insects continually traverse numerous roads in North America. Some species are actually attracted to highways (e.g., lovebugs), and others are lured by car headlights (e.g., moths). As a consequence, many insects are unintentionally hit by motorists. Fortunately (or unfortunately, depending on how you look at it), this event provides a unique opportunity to identify and learn about these wonderful creatures.

The purpose of this book is not only to help you to identify insects according to their "splats" (the distinctive residue they leave on your car), but to provide interesting facts about types of insects and activities you can do with them. I'll teach you how to observe insects in their natural environments and how to raise them at home.

For the curious person, this book contains ideas on how you can conduct scientific research in order to discover new things about insects. (Whoops! I said the "S" word.) Science (and scientists) sometimes give people a "creepy" feeling. Many folks believe that anything scientific must involve complicated contraptions and ideas that practically nobody can understand, or that only people with university degrees can conduct research. But anybody can be a scientist. Believe it or not, research is often fun and easy to do. All you need is an inquisitive mind.

This book also contains games for kids (as well as adults) to pass the time while driving down the road. I remember many family trips where, in addition to fighting with my brother in the back seat, we played an assortment of silly but fun games. I hope the games in this book will be added to your collection.

You may wonder how I collected data for this book. First, to get an idea of what types of splats are made by what types of insects, I spent most of my time at a Greyhound bus station in Gainesville. It was a perfect place to find a number of vehicles covered with squashed insects. These monstrous buses had a huge surface area, and traveled throughout the state of Florida. During some months, the front end was practically covered with splats! I had a fantastic time collecting specimens and I am indebted to the bus drivers and people that run the station. Many of the passengers thought it was unbelievable that I was actually picking dead bugs off the front of the bus. I heard quite a wide range of comments. Here are some of my favorites:

"What are ya goin' to do with them bugs.... smoke 'em?"

"When you're done, can you wax the front end too?"

"Mommy, why is that man scraping bugs off the windshield? Is he crazy?"

"He must be an archaeologist. No ... that's not right. What are those insect people called?"

"You must be one of them buggy people from the University. Cool!"

"No son, he's not a mechanic."

"What the #@!@# are ya doing? Yuuckk! That's gross!"*

"Are you sure you aren't psycho?"

Second, to gather additional information on insects encountered in other regions, I took a trip across the U.S. in the summer of '94. On May 8, strapped in my '84 Honda Accord, I ventured first from Gainesville to Boston, Massachusetts; next, I motored west through Detroit, Michigan, Chicago, Illinois, Rapid City, South Dakota, and eventually ended up in Seattle, Washington. From Seattle, I headed south through Portland, Oregon and Death Valley, California. Then I went east to Tucson, Arizona and continued back to Florida, stopping in Austin, Texas and Baton Rouge, Louisiana. Incidentally, I rigged the top portion of my car to collect insects that ricocheted off the windshield, so later I could match each splat with the appropriate insect. This apparatus is easy to build, and I explain how to construct it in the section on collecting and preserving insects. Two months, twelve thousand miles, and dozens of Greyhound Bus stations later, I had collected quite a number of insects and observed all types of splats in various regions of North America. In some areas, my windshield was almost covered with insect goo.

Driving through North America, I was struck by the sensation that I was watching a movie with my windshield posing as a big picture screen. The scenery whizzed by, changing with every hill conquered or turn navigated. At times, it felt like only the things in my car were real, and the outside stuff was fake. Yes, technology has brought us many wonderful things to make our lives easier, but unfortunately it has also isolated us from nature. Lewis Mumford, a noted urban ecologist, lamented over the technological advancement of humans. In *The Ecological City*, he describes one technological innovation, urban cities, as

> . . . a tendency to loosen the bonds that connect [the city's] inhabitants with nature and to transform, eliminate, or replace its earth-bound aspects, covering the natural site with an artificial environment that enhances the dominance of man and encourages an illusion of complete independence from nature.

Looking out the window of my car, watching a kaleidoscope of trees, meadows, streams, and mountains whiz by, I almost felt as if they were merely images in my mind. Only when I stopped, got out of my car, and hiked down a trail or tromped through a meadow, touching, smelling, and listening to nature did I realize that all of those images were real. They were not just figments of my imagination. These metallic creatures in which we travel from one place to another have essentially isolated us from the natural environment. We have all the comforts of home right at our fingertips: heat, air-conditioning, a comfortable chair, and music (sometimes playing quite loudly to drown out all outside noises). No wonder we may be lulled into thinking that the scenery outside our car is just cinema.

However, the sound and up-close view of some insect crashing into our windshield disrupts our view of this surreal world. Not only do some large insects make a loud "Bang!"—startling us out of our mesmerized state—but they leave behind gooey residues that ultimately, if enough insects strike the windshield, obstruct our view of the road. Pull into any filling station across North America and you will find a window washer especially designed to wash off the remains of those unfortunate insects that cling to the surface of the windshield. Do people think at all about the insects they are wiping off their cars?

The motivation to write this book came from my desire to communicate to people outside the scientific community about science, animals, and the natural environment in which we live. I chose to focus on local animals because I feel these critters are just as fascinating as those from faraway places. Folks of all ages can

"MOVE! Now! Now! Nowwwee!... BUS!...Aaakk... #@/*@#.."

identify with creatures they encounter everyday. People are naturally interested in animals and the environment, but the dilemma for scientists is how to effectively communicate to the public about the world around them and get them involved without being humdrum and boring? This question was on my mind just as I hit a large insect on a highway road.

I hope this book will not only spark interest about insects, but will increase people's awareness about their local environment. This guide can also be used as an education tool for teachers interested in teaching science. Take this book on any trip; I suggest placing the book in your glove compartment and when you have a "close encounter" with an insect, you can immediately identify and learn some interesting facts about it. Good luck and have a safe trip!

Mark Hostetler

Author's Note

If you would like to discuss anything or if you have some specific questions about insects (or any other animal-oriented subjects), I will gladly respond to your inquiries. Also, I enjoy receiving letters about people's experiences with insects or other animals and would love to put together a book on the subject. Please send a letter with a self-addressed, stamped envelope c/o Ten Speed Press (or you can e-mail me at hos@zoo.ufl.edu). Another way to contact me is through the Internet. I have a web page site at

http://nersp.nerdc.ufl.edu/~arm/people/hos.html.

I should stress that this book is applicable anywhere in North America (and even overseas). For example, a butterfly splat found on your windshield in Canada or Mexico will have the same characteristics as a butterfly splat in the United States. I even drove my car in Canada and the splats of each insect group were quite similar to the splats of the same insect group found in the U.S.

As an aside, I am trying to start a campaign to get rid of lawns and exotic vegetation from the private property of homeowners across North America. Manicured lawns and exotic vegetation are practically "concrete" to most natural species. In fact, because urban/suburban landscapes are becoming the dominant landscape type in North America, much of our natural wildlife will have a difficult time surviving in the near future. I strongly encourage people to redesign their landscape with native vegetation and to reduce the area required for mowing. (In other words, stop mowing in areas with low traffic; you will be pleasantly surprised what vegetation comes up!). As a collective group, we can reduce the impact on many animal species by simply designing landscapes naturally. Many endangered species (such as various Neotropical migrating birds) will feed in naturally designed backyard habitats. Just think of all the neat species you will get to observe firsthand in your yard!

INTRODUCTION

I n order to identify a splat, one section of the book has drawings and descriptions of various insect residues that you will probably encounter while driving down a road. Below these splats, a colorful illustration of an insect is provided to give you an idea of what it looked like before it smashed into your windshield. As you can imagine, I had a difficult time allocating one particular splat to a particular species. More often than not, I identified a splat to a group of insects (e.g., mosquitoes or cockroaches), rather than to a known species. When trying to identify a splat, keep in mind that a splat can be quite variable; however, each splat normally has several characteristics that are specific to a particular insect group, and I list the most prominent aspects of each particular splat. Look for similarities between the splat on your windshield and the description in this book. Also note the time of day, the season, and where you were when you hit the insect. This information, combined with the type of splat, will allow you to deduce which insect group it is in and possibly the species. For each group of insects, it should be kept in mind that every group contains quite a large number of insects with different sizes, shapes, and colors. Each illustration of an insect is just to show the general appearance of insects found in a group.

Another section of the book contains information about the insects you identify. I divided this section into four parts. First, I give some general information and some interesting stories about each insect group or species. Second, I provide the **Natural Life History**, or biological description of each insect. Most of this information is derived from the more common insects within a group since there are too many in each group to list all of them. Third, I give some fun things to do to help you discover more about the life of the insect you have just encountered. Fourth, I provide information and facts about common species that you will probably hit on the road (this will help you identify the splat). All of these parts, taken together, are meant to expose you to the fascinating world of insects!

Fun Things to Do sections contain activities you can do with insects, describes where you can find them in their natural habitat, and explains how you can recognize them. This part also includes some questions about the insects that can be answered by conducting experiments or basic observations. These activities and questions are not meant to be limiting. As you will soon see, the more you find out about insects, the more questions you will have. Some of the information you will discover may be quite interesting to scientists; you might even be able to publish some of your findings in a scientific journal.

When designing an experiment, be sure to take into account all other factors that may influence an experiment. For example, let's say you want to know if mosquitoes are attracted to carbon dioxide. You have a cage full of mosquitoes, and you decide to run an experiment by placing a cloth infused with carbon dioxide on one side of the cage. Your intention is simply to observe the number of mosquitoes that land on the cloth. However, if mosquitoes do land on this cloth, you cannot conclude that mosquitoes are attracted to carbon dioxide without eliminating other possibilities.

Many other factors may have contributed to mosquitoes landing on the cloth. For instance, mosquitoes may simply prefer the side of the cage containing the treated cloth, not the treated cloth itself. To determine if mosquitoes have such a bias, run a control experiment by placing two cloths on each side of the cage. An equal number of mosquitoes should land on each cloth. Also, the cloth's texture, odor, or color may have attracted the mosquitoes, not carbon dioxide. To control for these other possibilities, place an additional cloth on the other side of the cage when conducting this experiment. This control cloth should be identical in every way to the treated cloth except that it does not contain carbon dioxide. Keep in mind, this particular experiment does not rule out the possibility that the cloth's texture, odor, or color also attracts mosquitoes. You are simply testing the effect of carbon dioxide on the behavior of mosquitoes.

Repeat the test a number of times with new mosquitoes, and randomly switch the position of the cloths in the cage. If the mosquitoes continue to land on the treated cloth, this will give you more confidence that carbon dioxide attracts mosquitoes. Additionally, it is important to know as much as you can about an organism's biology before designing an experiment. For example, if mosquitoes are only active at night, the above experiments may not work during the day.

Remember, when conducting an experiment, the idea is to isolate what you are testing for by controlling any external factors. Some parting advice: think like the organism you are studying. Above all, have fun!

Common Insects Hit by Cars and Trucks sections contain those insects or groups of insects you are most likely to hit in various regions of North America. I placed a box ($\square$) next to these common species so you can check them off as you encounter them. Most insects listed in this book can be found on windshields of cars throughout North America; however, in some cases, I describe a few notable species that only occur in certain regions of the U.S. (e.g., Northeast, Southeast, Northwest, and Southwest). The Canadian and Mexican areas that border these regions should also contain the listed species. I provide specifics about where and when you would encounter these insects and information about the eggs, larvae, and adults. In addition, I list a couple of the smaller insects that are impossible to collect from windshields (they don't leave behind enough body parts to identify). I wrote about them anyway because they probably represent the smallest splats found on windshields. Please note that bug measurements are given in milimeters (mm) and centimeters (cm). There are 25.4 mm and 2.54 cm in 1 inch.

You will notice that after the common name for each insect or insect group, some weird-looking words follow. This is Latin, and it is used to give organisms and groups of organisms internationally recognizable names. Using a common language avoids the confusion that happens when organisms are given names in different languages. Further, Latin names are very precise. Common names used for an organism may actually include several species. For instance, the term "palmetto bug" encompasses several different species of cockroaches. In this book, when a common name of an insect is given, the scientific name follows in italics (i.e., Honey bees *Apis mellifera*). Scientific names are binomial, which means "two names." Thus, for honey bees, *Apis* is the genus (or generic name), and *Apis mellifera* is the species (or specific name).

Further, most insects in the table of contents are placed under a broad classification called an order. Insects may also be placed under more specific categories, such as a family, genus, or species. Wherever I indicate "spp," that insect could be several species. "But," you ask, "what the heck is an order, family, genus, or species?" These are taxonomic categories from a scientific filing system called taxonomy created by a Swedish physician and botanist, Carolus Linnaeus, in the eighteenth century. This filing system is a way of grouping similar-looking animals into separate categories. Organisms are placed in different categories depending on certain morphological characteristics (such as the shape of a wing or a leg). Scientists place organisms into increasingly more specific categories:

K i n g d o m
P h y l u m
C l a s s
O r d e r
Family
Genus
Species

Starting from the most specific category and working our way up the list, above, similar species are grouped in the same genus, similar genera (plural for genus) are placed in the same family, similar families into orders, orders into classes, classes into phyla (plural for phylum), and phyla into kingdoms (the broadest category). For example, all the insects in this book are grouped into the class Insecta (i.e., animals that have three pairs of legs, antennae, and three distinct body regions (head, thorax, abdomen), phylum Arthropoda (i.e., animals that have an exoskeleton), and kingdom Animalia (i.e., organisms that eat other organisms for nourishment). Thus both humans and insects are classified under the kingdom Animalia (the most general category), but humans are not grouped under the phylum Arthropoda (a more specific category which contains only animals with exoskeletons). A good way to remember the taxonomic categories is to use the mnemonic, "King Phillip's Car Often Finds Gunk Splats!"

Last but not least, throughout the sections, I frequently ask questions that may or may not have a particular answer. They are meant solely to be thought provoking, not distressing. Many of these questions are even difficult for a trained scientist to answer!

·ANTS·

ORDER: HYMENOPTERA
FAMILY: FORMICIDAE

I know what you're thinking . . . how the heck can you hit an ant with your windshield when they crawl on the ground? Well, some ants in a colony are born with wings. These ants are called alates. Being primarily dispersers, these winged ants of both sexes leave their home colonies to establish new colonies. The number of ants during mating flights can be quite high, and thousands are hit by cars on the road.

Ants are everywhere and one is hard pressed to find an area that does not contain them. They have been around for a very long time. Judging from fossil records, ants were quite numerous in the early Tertiary period, approximately fifty million years ago. Preserved ants from this period can be found in bits of amber, which is the fossilized resin of pine trees. Ants were trapped in this sticky substance and subsequently preserved for millions of years. Do you have any amber? Look closely inside a piece, and you will probably see parts of an ant or even a whole ant. This is a good way to tell fake amber from real. Just think, ants found inside amber are approximately fifty million years old!

Like wasps and bees, ants are very social and every individual is assigned a particular duty. Each colony normally has at least one queen that lays all the eggs. The typical ant we see everyday is a worker ant, an infertile female that hatched from a fertilized egg. Workers conduct a wide variety of activities such as foraging, constructing nests, looking after eggs and larvae, feeding the queen, guarding the colony, and raiding nearby ant colonies.

Have you ever been on a picnic and left out a bit of food that was quickly discovered by a large number of ants? If you looked closely, you saw the ants formed a trail leading right up to the food. How do they find it so fast? You might think ants have an incredible sense of smell, but in fact they cannot smell beyond a centimeter or so. Given that they cannot smell very far, how do so many ants find a piece of food in such a short period of time?

Ants have a quick way of communicating to each other when they find a good source of food. When one of the many "scouts" accidentally bumps into some food and discovers she is not able to carry all of it herself, she goes back to the nest and tells the rest of the colony. On the way to the nest, the scout lays down a scent trail for the rest of the ants to follow. Once inside the nest, the scout runs around excitedly, bumping into other ants and spreading the smell of the food. Then, lots of ants exit the nest and follow the scent trail back to the food. This is the trail that we see. Ants have receptors on their antennae that detect the scent trail.

Natural Life History of Ants

Ants eat almost everything, depending on the species and what is available in the area surrounding the nest. However some ants are specialists and only feed on one type of food. For example, several species feed primarily on the excretion of aphids. This substance is called honeydew. An ant will "milk" an aphid by tickling its rear end, stimulating the aphid to produce a small honeydew droplet that is very nutritious for the ant. Ants will even herd aphids and protect them from potential predators (kind of like farmers, eh?).

Ant nests consist mainly of infertile workers, but during a particular time of the year, a portion of the eggs will receive larger amounts of food, and these eggs will develop into winged adults (alates). Females hatch from fertilized eggs, whereas males hatch from unfertilized eggs.

Winged adults leave the nest in hopes of establishing a new colony. Males of some species form swarms and wait for females to fly through them in order to mate. Flying swarms are attacked by many creatures, such as birds, mammals, and large insects. Here is a tough question: why do most species of ants mate away from the nest? Why don't females mate with males inside the nest before dispersing? (Hint: it has to do with increasing genetic variation.)

Once mated, a queen loses her wings in three to five days and begins laying eggs in a new location. It is difficult for queens to start a new nest from scratch. Most gain entrance into an existing nest of their own species and begin laying eggs there. Queens do not normally forage for food once they have found an appropriate site. To raise the first brood, they depend primarily on their reserves accumulated from the larval stage. The first daughter workers are born in about sixty days. As soon as they hatch, workers forage for food, feed the queen and her larvae, and enlarge the nest. However, only a small percentage of the first generation of workers actually mature. Apparently some of the larvae feed on the other eggs laid within the nest.

Surprisingly, some queens are known to take over nests of other species! For example, *Formica rufa* are known to take over nests of *Formica fusca*! They do this in a very sneaky way. Queens gain entrance into a nest either by offering food to the guard ants (humans are not the only animals that bribe!) or sometimes by fighting with a few guard ants and in the process, obtaining the scent of the colony. Thus, upon returning to the nest, she smells like members of the colony and is allowed to enter. When familiar with the nest, the new queen finds the other queen and promptly bites her head off. (Yikes!) The new queen then lays eggs of her own species, and the workers of the colony are duped into raising these eggs as their own. Eventually, the new queen's progeny replace the other genera.

Fun Things to Do with Ants

You can observe the behaviors of ants in any backyard. Drop pieces of food near an ant nest and time how long it takes for them to discover it. What happens when a scout comes across the piece of food? Does it attempt to drag it back to the nest? Ants are really strong for their size. See how big a piece of food an ant can carry.

Time how long it takes for more ants to discover a piece of food and then put an obstacle in their path. How long does it take before they negotiate it? What part of the ant do you think "smells" the scent trails?

Ant cages can be very interesting to build because you can watch the behavior of ants while they are underground. Because of their social behavior, ants will always be doing something different in various parts of the cage. Cages can be bought or built (refer to pages 104–108 for a list of references, in particular *An Introduction to the Study of Insects* by J. B. Borror, D. M. Delong, and C. A. Triplehorn).

Common Ants Hit by Cars and Trucks

☐ THE CARPENTER ANT (Genus: *Camponotus*)

Local distribution:

Alates are encountered on most roads at night from May to July.

Eggs and larvae:

Eggs and larvae are found in nests that are located in wood objects (such as logs).

Adults:

Adults are quite common in the summer and spring, near sources of wood.

Interesting facts:

Carpenter ants are large (12.5 to 18.75 mm in length) and have a reddish head and thorax; the abdomen is dark. These ants build nests in wood by excavating an assortment of chambers with their strong mandibles (mouth parts). Unlike termites, carpenter ants do not eat wood. They feed on other insects, honeydew, and a variety of seeds. They all are very partial to any sweet tidbit left by humans in their homes.

Although carpenter ants do not inflict a sting as painful as fire ants, they can still hurt! A threatened ant will first bite you with its mandibles and then spray formic acid on the wound (they don't actually have a stinger).

☐ THE FIRE ANT (*Solenopsis invicta*)

Local distribution:

Alates are encountered on most roads during the day intermittently through the year.

Eggs and larvae:

Eggs and larvae are found mostly underground in nests which can reach 60 cm above ground.

Adults:

Adults are common year-round, and nests are in almost every landscape-disturbed area.

Interesting facts:

Although there is a native American fire ant species (*Solenopsis geminata*), by far the most common fire ant is the imported fire ant (*Solenopsis invicta*). This species is originally from South America and was introduced into Florida in the 1920s. It subsequently spread throughout the Southeast. These ants are incredibly good at producing huge numbers of alates and establishing new nests. One researcher found 186,000 female alates in one acre! A number of birds and other insects take advantage of mating flights to gobble up a few winged fire ants. But there are so many alates, that a few fertilized queens always escape to start new colonies. These queens burrow into the ground and lay ten to thirty eggs. A queen feeds her larvae with her own bodily resources; the emergent workers forage and expand the size of the nest. It takes approximately two to three years before a colony begins to produce alates, and mature nests may contain 100,000 individuals!

Beware! The fire ant can inflict a fiery, painful sting, which will continue to burn for several minutes. Even though these ants are small (less than 6.25 mm in length), humans and animals alike give wide berth to fire ant nests. When a nest is disturbed, fire ants swarm around and repeatedly sting the helpless intruder.

To control fire ant populations, you can buy over-the-counter bait formulations. Follow directions precisely, and keep in mind that it will take three to four weeks before you see any results. You will probably have to repeat the treatment in the near future. I strongly suggest treating your property only when you have an unusual number of fire ant nests. If you treat your whole property for only a few nests, you will most likely kill more native ant species, and this will make it easier for fire ants to invade your property.

· ANTLIONS ·

ORDER: NEUROPTERA
FAMILY: MYRMELEONTIDAE

Antlion larvae are strange-looking creatures that sometimes construct circular pits in the sand. People often notice these dimples in the sand, frequently located under the eaves of houses, but do not know that antlion larvae produce these pits to trap other insects. Equipped with long mandibles (mouthparts), antlion larvae hide out at the bottom of these pits and grab any unlucky insect that happens to tumble in. People in the south call these insects "doodlebugs" (because of the way they leave tracks in the sand), and one entomologist even nicknamed them "demons of the dust." Not all antlion larvae build pits. Some species hide out in the surface of the sand and catch unsuspecting insects that wander by. In fact, twenty-two species of antlion have been identified in the state of Florida. Some species can even be found in dry tree hollows and cave mouths.

Not many people have seen antlion larvae, and almost nobody recognizes the adults, which are small, winged insects that resemble lacewings. It is amazing that antlion larvae, any ant's worst nightmare, become delicate-looking, flying adults. Larvae that construct the familiar sand pits are in the genus *Myrmeleon*, and their pits literally dot the landscape in sandy areas of the Southeast.

Natural Life History of Antlions

Not much is known about the life cycle of antlions. What the eggs look like or where they are laid is a mystery. However, larvae are readily observed because of the pitfall traps some species construct. Other species frequently leave trails in the sand.

Depending on how often they feed, antlion larvae become adults in one to two years. Both larvae and adults are predators. Larvae feed on insects that crawl on the ground (e.g., ants), and adults feed on caterpillars and aphids found in bushes.

Fun Things to Do with Antlions

Antlion larvae are fun to watch and play with. Have you ever caught an ant and dropped it into an antlion pit to see what happens? While the struggling ant tries to crawl up the sides, the antlion throws sand up at the ant, trying to knock it back down. It is truly a race to see whether the ant gets out in time before the antlion grabs it!

It is easy to catch a few antlion larvae, and you can use an aquarium (or some type of box) to house these critters. Antlion larvae are found in sandy areas under building eaves. To catch them, pound on the ground right next to the pit and the larvae will sometimes surface, or quickly scoop up the entire pit and sift through the sand to locate the antlion. Careful, antlion larvae are difficult to see. You will have better success if you have a small sieve. Do not worry, antlion larvae do not bite.

Help!... we've fallen and we can't get out...

When you are raising antlions, place a net over the top of the container so you can catch the adults. Adult antlions look totally different from the larval form. When the adults appear, provide them with some vegetation that has caterpillars or aphids on it. Feed antlion larvae ants (be sure to immobilize them so they don't crawl out of the container). Also, take notes! How many ants can a larvae eat in one week? Do the larvae construct cocoons? If they do, how long do they remain in the cocoon? When do the adults emerge from the cocoon? Is there any kind of courtship between antlion adults?

If you are lucky, you might even get a female to oviposit (lay eggs). What do the eggs look like and where did she lay them? In the sand or on the vegetation? How long does it take for the larvae to hatch out? All of your observations could be important to entomologists.

You can also catch adults at night with shining bright lights. They have four similarly shaped wings, so be careful! It is easy to confuse them with lacewings!

Common Antlions Hit by Cars and Trucks

☐ **COMMON ANTLIONS (Family: Myrmeleontidae)**

Local distribution:

These insects are encountered primarily on roads in the South at night, in the spring, summer, and fall (they sometimes appear in the North).

Eggs and larvae:

Larvae (in the genus *Myrmeleon*) construct pitfall traps in the sand.

Adults:

Adults are large (40 to 80 mm in length) with delicate wings, and resemble lacewings.

· BITING MIDGES ·
(NO-SEE-UMS)
ORDER: DIPTERA
FAMILY: CERATOPOGONIDAE

Many people also call these insects "sand flies" and are familiar with the painful bites they inflict. They live around coastal beaches, but hardly anyone actually sees them. Some species can be as small as .5 mm. Only females bite because they require blood for egg maturation. There are over five hundred species in North America. Many species bite humans (primarily belonging to the genera *Culicoides* and *Leptoconops*), but other species also attack dragonflies, mantids, lacewings, and even mosquitoes. A biting midge will track down a female mosquito engorged with blood and suck a little of it out of her abdomen . . . what retribution! The biter getting bit!

One researcher, D. S. Kettle, said about sand flies, "one midge is an entomological curiosity, a thousand can be hell. . . ."

Natural Life History of Biting Midges

These insects are no larger than 1 mm, but they pack a powerful punch! Different species of biting midges often prefer certain hosts, such as live-stock, deer, rabbits, birds, and even humans. Both sexes feed on flower nectar and live for about two weeks.

The mating habits of biting midges are similar to black flies. Males of most species form swarms and wait for females to fly through the swarm. Other species mate at a feeding site. For example, some males hang out around a cow and mate with incoming females seeking blood. Males "hear" females with their plume-like antennae, detecting flying females

What an entomological curiosity!

by the frequency of their wing beat. Males have only a short time in which to mate; they are usually past their prime after only eight hours. Older males (24 to 36 hrs) are often rebuffed by females who deem them too "elderly!"

Females oviposit (lay eggs) in a variety of places, but every site must have a minimal amount of moisture or the eggs will not survive. Some deposit eggs in sandy soil, small streams, salt marshes, intertidal zones, mangrove swamps, and even in moist leaf litter or manure. Eggs hatch in a few days, and larvae feed on organic debris and small organisms, such as protozoans. Aquatic larvae must come to the surface to acquire oxygen. They are also important prey to other larger insect larvae.

Fun Things to Do with Biting Midges

Using yourself as bait, capture a few females, bring them home, and place them in a cage. You can also trap males at night with light traps. You can do experiments similar to those mentioned in the mosquito section. What is so attractive about humans? Try different stimuli, such as color, heat, and carbon dioxide. Test members in your family: which one is the most attractive to biting midges? Are there any differences when compared to mosquitoes? You may even discover an effective repellent against these biters!

If you can get a female to lay her eggs, observe what the larvae look like and their behavior (you will need a microscope). You might see some unusual interactions among the larvae.

Common Biting Midges Hit by Cars and Trucks

☐ **COMMON BITING MIDGES (Family: Ceratopogonidae)**

Local distribution:

These insects are encountered on most roads in the spring, summer, and fall.

Eggs and larvae:

Found in various moist areas.

Adults:

Adults are small and difficult to see.

· BLACK FLIES ·

ORDER: DIPTERA
FAMILY: SIMULIIDAE

Many a fisherman, boater, or swimmer is well-acquainted with these sometimes vicious little biters. Swarms composed of both males and females often form about your head. The adults are no larger than 5 mm, and only females are bloodsuckers. Incongruous to their size, however, their bite is really painful and can cause swelling and itching. Black flies, unlike mosquitoes (which insert needlelike mouthparts to obtain blood), lacerate the skin with serrated mouthparts and suck up the blood that oozes from the wound.

But where do you think black flies lay their eggs? Rotting organic matter? Nope. Almost all species deposit their eggs in fast-moving, clean water. The larvae are entirely aquatic.

I vant to suck your blooood!

Black flies do not carry any type of disease in the United States, but two species in Africa carry a worm that causes onchoceriasis (river blindness) in humans. Whenever there is an outbreak, researchers search local rivers to find where the larvae live and exterminate them. The search proved to be quite difficult for one species, *S. neavei*, which was not found anywhere in several rivers in areas where onchoceriasis occurred. Researchers began to think that the larvae were lodged in the bodies of other aquatic organisms. After searching a variety of such animals for three weeks (including the larvae of caddisflies, stoneflies, mayflies, and different species of fish and crabs), the larvae were discovered on a species of crab. Wow! Can you believe these flies complete their larval stage while hitchhiking on crabs? I wonder how the larvae locate the crabs.

Natural Life History of Black Flies

Adult males and females feed on a variety of sugar sources (i.e., flower nectar), but females feed on blood to produce offspring. Males of some species swarm for mating purposes, whereas others search for females independently. Swarming males use several markers (i.e., a branch) in order to keep the same position while flying around. Thus, even when they scatter, males can return to the same spot. What are the advantages and disadvantages of forming a swarm? One possible advantage is that swarms attract more females than if each male were to search separately. However, I bet dragonflies, which would not hesitate to feast on black flies, easily detect these swarms! I wager the males scatter pretty fast when a dragonfly is around.

After mating, a female lays her eggs in fast-moving water by periodically dipping her abdomen into it. Females of some species even crawl under the water to lay eggs! Eggs of most species have a sticky outer covering, so they quickly attach to vegetation or sink to the bottom of the stream. Larvae are completely aquatic (they do not come to the surface for air) and are filter-feeders, attaching themselves to solid objects, picking out organic debris that floats by. Most species of black flies hatch in huge numbers in the spring, but by midsummer, most adults are gone (thank goodness, eh?).

Fun Things to Do with Black Flies

Although larvae are difficult to rear (because an aquarium needs to be highly oxygenated), you can easily catch adult flies. Use yourself as bait and pretty soon you will have a bunch of females swarming around you. Take the flies home and place them in a cage. You can do experiments similar to those mentioned in the mosquito section. What is so attractive about humans? Try different stimuli such as color, heat, and carbon dioxide. Test members of your family and friends: who is the most attractive to black flies? Are there any differences when compared to mosquitoes? You may even discover an effective repellent against these insects.

Common Black Flies Hit by Cars and Trucks

☐ **COMMON BLACK FLIES (Family: Simuliidae)**

Local Distribution:

These insects are encountered on most roads in spring, summer, and fall.

Eggs and larvae:

Found in fast-moving streams. The larvae, which hang out in groups, are black.

Adults:

Adults are small, compact, and have a humpbacked appearance.

BUTTERFLIES AND MOTHS

ORDER: LEPIDOPTERA

People are quite familiar with colorful butterflies fluttering in the sunlight, and at night people recognize moths flying crazily around light bulbs. But what is the difference between moths and butterflies?

There is a common misconception that moth wings are not as colorful as butterfly wings and that moths fly only at night. In fact, some species of moths are even more colorful than most butterflies and several species of moths fly during the day. So how can you tell the difference between the two? One characteristic that differentiates them is the shape of their antennae: moths have antennae that are hairy, sawtoothed, or shaped like a feather. In contrast, butterfly antennae are smooth with knobs on the end. Take a close look the next time you spot a butterfly or moth.

The wing of a butterfly or moth is an incredible collection of different-colored scales arranged in a specific way. Put a wing under a microscope and you will see quite an amazing pattern! If you touch a butterfly or moth wing, a bunch of "dust" will cover your fingers. This dust is actually scales.

Have you ever wondered why moths fly crazily around lights, smashing themselves into the bright bulbs? You might think to yourself, "What a stupid moth!" Well, let's place ourselves in the "shoes" of a moth. For thousands of years, moths have been using the moon to orient themselves while flying at night. To fly in a straight line, moths fly at a particular angle to the moonlight (usually less than 90 degrees). Because the moon is so far away, all moonlight rays are parallel to each other. Thus, when moths fly at a constant angle to parallel moonlight beams, they end up traveling in a straight line.

"But," you ask, "why is it important to travel in a straight line?" One hypothesis is that when a moth wants to cover a long distance to find another habitat (or even a potential mate), it is more efficient to travel in a straight line than zig-zagging back and forth. A moth flying about randomly would not get very far. Think about a male moth that is searching for the pheromone plume (scent trail) of a female moth. If it traveled around in circles, it would have less of a chance of picking up the scent of a female than a male moth that traveled in a straight line and covered more distance. What a clever mechanism moths have to orient themselves at night.

This form of orientation was a practical way for moths to travel at night until Thomas Edison came along and invented the light bulb. Suddenly, artificial lights were everywhere and moths began to encounter what they believed were moonbeams but were actually artificial rays of light coming from bulbs at different angles. As a moth encounters an artificial ray of light, it alters its flight pattern to keep a constant angle to each ray. If that angle is less than 90 degrees, the moth circles around the light and eventually begins to spin closer and closer to the source, smashing itself into the light bulb. Can you imagine the number of moths that have died from this action? I have a sneaking suspicion that some species of moths have now altered their orienting mechanism. For instance, if a moth flies at an angle greater than 90 degrees, it would spin away from light bulbs! It would be neat to discover a species of moth that has switched its flight-orienting mechanism because of the dangers of flying into light bulbs!

Many types of frogs, toads, and geckos gather around lights to obtain an easy meal. Go out on your porch and I'll bet you will find a toad hanging out by the light, snatching up moths that come too close.

Natural Life History of Butterflies and Moths

Almost everyone is familiar with the process of metamorphosis in butterflies and moths: egg, larva, pupa, adult. This transformation seems almost magical! Below is a brief description of how butterfly and moth eggs transform into beautiful, flying adults.

First, eggs are usually laid by adults on the leaves of a plant that the larvae can later feed on. A waxy layer covers the outside of the eggs to prevent water loss. Eggs will hatch within five to twenty days, depending on the weather and the species.

After hatching, larvae (caterpillars) are virtual eating machines. They consume vast amounts of food. In only a few weeks, some species will increase their weight as much as ten thousand times! Caterpillars come in all sizes, shapes, and colors. Some are brightly colored while others seem to match the color of the leaves they are eating, making them difficult to see.

Butterflies -- the original transformers!

Why do you think some species advertise themselves while others hide? Colorful species that advertise their presence are usually toxic to a predator and taste bad whereas camouflaged species hide because they would be a scrumptious snack. For example, the toxic monarch caterpillar (*Danaus plexippus*) is bright yellow, black, and white; a tasty giant swallowtail caterpillar (*Heraclides cresphontes*) resembles a bird dropping when it is small (not many birds eat bird droppings, eh?). Monarch caterpillars are poisonous because they eat milkweed plants, which contain toxic substances. The toxin absorbed by the caterpillar does not affect it, but any bird that eats the toxic caterpillar will become ill and throw up. It doesn't take many taste tests for birds to learn to avoid yellow, black, and white caterpillars.

Why do you think some caterpillars are hairy? Well, don't you think twice before picking one up, because it might sting you? Also, a hairy caterpillar may not be palatable because the hairs probably irritate the linings of bird stomachs.

When a caterpillar is ready to pupate, a moth caterpillar will spin a cocoon (a covering made of silk), and a butterfly caterpillar will form a chrysalis (a hard, shiny shell) that is suspended by a small ball of silk from a branch. Cocoons and chrysalides protect the changing caterpillars from outside forces such as wind and rain.

When an adult emerges, it must first rest and pump fluid into its wings. The transformation takes several minutes and when the wings harden, the adult is ready to fly away. Almost all moths and butterflies feed on the nectar of flowers with a long coiled tube called a proboscis.

Plants benefit from feeding moths and butterflies because these insects inadvertently transport pollen from plant to plant, completing fertilization. Think about it: colorful, sweet-smelling flowers are not just for our enjoyment; they are made by plants primarily to attract butterflies and other pollinators. In addition to feeding on flowers, many species of butterflies will feed on rotting fruits or even decomposed frogs smashed on roads (yummy!).

Adult butterflies and moths are cold-blooded, so when the air is cool, they need to find a place to warm up. In the morning, butterflies will seek out sunny areas and spread their wings in order to soak up as much sun as possible. Because most moths are nocturnal, they must resort to muscular activity in order to warm up. Like you or me, when moths are cold, they will shiver to elevate their body temperature.

Moths and butterflies, like all animals, seek out members of the opposite sex in order to reproduce. Male butterflies will patrol areas in which females feed and hang out. To attract males, the female releases a chemical scent (called a pheromone) which the male picks up with his antennae. The scent can travel quite a long distance and males will follow the trail all the way back to a female. If you see a daytime species of moth careening crazily around your yard, he may be hotly pursuing the scent of a female!

Fun Things to Do with Butterflies and Moths

A most enjoyable activity is the observation of butterflies in their natural habitat. Equipped with binoculars, you can observe their feeding and mating habits. What species of plants do butterflies visit? Some of your observations may be unique because field guides typically do not indicate every plant species that each butterfly feeds on. Do they feed in groups or as individuals? With luck, you may be able to see a few mating rituals (sometimes several males will have a dogfight in the air to gain access to a female). If you get up early in the morning, you can get close enough to some butterflies (because they are cold) to take some excellent pictures.

To attract moths, you can place a dish outside containing a mixture of sugar with beer, molasses, or fruit (add a little yeast to promote fermentation). You will be pleasantly surprised by the number of pretty moths that visit your bait. Place the dish outside on a platform just at dusk, but make sure you remove it before morning or the ants and flies will get to it. Also, as discussed earlier, any bright, white light will attract a great number of moths.

I think a fun project would be to determine which species of moths are attracted to porch light bulbs. You can hang out around a light bulb and catch a variety of moths with a net. Which species seems to be most attracted to artificial light? Try and catch moths away from lights with a bait or a net. Are the same species caught at this location? Place several moth species in a cage with a light bulb and observe which species fly directly at the bulb. Do they ever give up?

Many people see a caterpillar and wonder what type of butterfly or moth it will become. It is a spectacular sight to see a larva pupate and then hatch out as an adult! Below are a few tips on how to collect and raise larvae successfully.

First, when you find a caterpillar, place it in a box for transportation with a few of the leaves it was eating or crawling on. Also, place a bunch of leaves in a separate container that contains some moisture so the leaves will not wilt on the way home. Be sure to note where the leaves were collected so you can return for more as needed.

Once home, obtain a gallon glass jar or any transparent container. Place a layer of moist towels on the bottom, then arrange the stems and leaves from the bottom to the top of the container. You need to have a lid that fits tightly to prevent the plant food from drying out, and each day, you should clean out the droppings and replenish the food. Opening the lid each day while cleaning the container will provide the caterpillar with enough oxygen to live. You can also construct a round rearing cage by attaching some screening (the type you put over windows) to pizza pans placed on the top and bottom. In this cage, place the ends of a branch of leaves into a jar of water covered by plastic wrap or some other material. The water will keep the leaves fresh and the plastic covering will prevent the caterpillar from drowning. Be sure to take careful notes about the appearance of the caterpillar and the adult moth or butterfly that emerges. You can ultimately make your own guide on moths and butterflies.

If you catch a pregnant moth or butterfly (difficult to tell, but they usually have large abdomens), place the moth or butterfly in a paper bag that has a wadded paper towel in it (for moths) or some preferred leaves for butterfly food. Most species will usually lay their eggs in a few days. The eggs can be found inside the paper towel, on the sides of the bag, or on the leaves. Sometimes, though, you might have to provide a female moth with a piece of bark from a preferred tree to induce her to lay eggs.

Collecting and preserving insects is fun, but is it harmful to species as a whole? For the most part, collecting a few moths or butterflies will not appreciably affect their respective population sizes; however, some species are on the Federal List of Endangered Species (e.g., Schaus's swallowtail in the Florida Keys), and one should not collect them. You can collect common butterflies on private property, but it is illegal to collect butterflies in state parks without a permit. You can build quite a collection of butterflies and moths, and these collections can be useful as teaching tools in schools and museums. When collecting, be sure to note the date and location of each butterfly and moth you collected (see the section on collecting and mounting insects, page 99).

Common Butterflies and Moths Hit by Cars and Trucks

☐ GEOMETER MOTHS (Family: Geometridae)

Local distribution:

These moths are encountered on most roads at night during warm months.

Eggs and larvae:

Larvae are familiar to most people as inchworms.

Adults:

Normally found in deciduous woodland.

Interesting facts:

This moth family has caterpillars that are commonly called measuring worms or inchworms. If the caterpillars are alarmed, they will stand erect and motionless, resembling small twigs. Why do you think they do this?

There are over 1,400 species in North America. These moths are slender-bodied, and their wings are often marked with fine wavy lines. Some larvae species are significant pests to trees (e.g., cankerworms). Most species are attracted to light and you will probably hit a lot of them on the road at night.

If you are familiar with biology, a European species in this family (*Biston betularae*—alias, "the pepper moth") is mentioned as a classic study of natural selection in most textbooks. Light-colored pepper moths were replaced by dark-colored moths when tree trunks were covered by black soot from nearby industrial plants (the trees were normally covered with white lichen). Why do you think dark forms replaced the white forms?

☐ NOCTUID MOTHS (Family: Noctuidae)

Local distribution:

These moths are encountered on most roads at night during warm months.

Eggs and larvae:

Larvae are smooth and dull-colored.

Adults:

Found almost everywhere.

Interesting facts:

Over 2,700 North American species of moths occur in this family. They are common, nocturnal, and most species are attracted to light. Adults can be quite colorful and many species are pests to crops. At rest, the wings are held flat or rooflike over the body. The corn earworm, *Heliothis zea*, is commonly found in ears of corn, and it also feeds on tomatoes and cotton.

☐ SNOUT AND GRASS MOTHS (Family: Pyralidae)

Local distribution:

These moths are encountered on most roads at night during warm months.

Eggs and larvae:

Eggs and larvae are found on many plants.

Adults:

Normally found in meadows and grasslands.

Interesting facts:

Over 1,100 North American species exist in this family. These moths are quite delicate and have a scaled proboscis (a long tube-like structure used for feeding). Larvae of many species are major pests to cereals, crops, nuts, and stored food supplies. One species, *Galleria mellonella*, lives in bee hives and feeds on bees wax!

Moths in the genus *Crambus* are quite common in meadows. They are recognizable by their pale yellowish-brown or whitish wings and their small size. The larvae of some species are known as sodworms, and feed on grasses at night.

☐ TORTRICID MOTHS (Family: Tortricidae)

Local distribution:

These moths are encountered on most roads at night during warm months.

Eggs and larvae:

Eggs and larvae are found on many plants.

Adults:

Normally found in deciduous woodland or orchards.

Interesting facts:

Over 1,000 North American species exist in this family. These moths are small and either tan, gray, or brown, with mottled areas on the wings. Most tortricid larvae are leaf tiers or leaf rollers—they fold or roll a leaf over themselves and hold this makeshift shelter together with bits of silk. The larvae of some species are significant pests to fruits. Oriental fruit moth larvae, *Grapholitha molesta*, for example bore into peaches and other fruits. Another tortricid larvae, the spruce budworm (*Choristoneura fumiferana*), is a big-time pest to spruce trees and other evergreens in the New England area and in some parts of the Canadian Boreal forest. During severe outbreaks of the spruce budworm, thousands and thousands of acres of forest have been destroyed. Little larva, mighty foe.

Another species, *Lydia deshaisiana*, has the larvae that gives the Mexican jumping bean its name. The larvae lives inside the seeds of a particular plant, and when disturbed, it throws itself against the inside wall, causing the bean to jump!

☐ EASTERN TIGER SWALLOWTAIL (*Heraclides glaucus*) and
☐ WESTERN TIGER SWALLOWTAIL (*Heraclides rutulus*)

Local distribution:

These butterflies are encountered on most roads during the day from March to November.

Eggs and larvae:

Eggs are greenish and spherical. They are normally found singly on stems and leaves, and hatch within seven days. Larvae are green and have an orange eye spot with a black pupil. Older larvae are browner.

Adults:

Normally found in deciduous woodland and along roads, streams, and rivers.

Interesting facts:

This species of butterfly is easily recognizable. It is a large, yellow and black butterfly with tails on the hind wings. This swallowtail is attracted to lilacs. Larvae can be found on tulip, basswood, cotton-wood, and willow trees.

The tiger swallowtail has several clever methods of evading predators. Some adult females are black with yellow spots on the hind wing. It is thought that these black females may be mimicking the coloration of pipevine swallowtails (*Battus philenor*), which are noxious to most birds. Black tiger swallowtails, although edible, escape being eaten by birds because they resemble pipevine swal-lowtails. In the early stages, caterpillars are black with a white mark across the back—resembling a bird dropping. What bird would eat bird poop? As they get bigger, caterpillars turn green and have an orange eye spot with a black pupil on the back. When disturbed, a bright-orange, forked gland on the top of the head flicks in and out . . . almost like a snake's tongue.

☐ SPICEBUSH BUTTERFLY (*Pterourus troilus*)

Local distribution:

Spicebush butterflies are primarily encountered during the day in the North and Southeastern regions of North America from March to November. They can also be found in eastern Texas, eastern Kansas, and Montana. I collected quite a few of these butterflies from Greyhound buses in the Northeast.

Eggs and larvae:

Larvae feed on sassafras, sweet bay, and prickly ash. Larvae are greenish with four orange eye spots (two with black pupils).

Adults:

Found in fields and edges of forests.

Interesting facts:

Older spicebush caterpillars are similar to tiger swallowtail caterpillars. They have orange eye spots with black pupils. When disturbed, they flick out a forked gland on the top of the head. They also release a scent that smells like rotten fruit.

☐ MONARCH BUTTERFLY (*Danaus plexippus*)

Local distribution:

Because monarchs migrate, they are most abundant in the South and the North at various times of the year. In the South, monarchs are primarily encountered on roads during the day from April to May, and September to November. In the North, monarchs are abundant from late April to October.

Eggs and larvae:

Eggs are yellow and located on the underside of milkweed leaves. Larvae are marked with white, black, and yellow bands and they molt four times. Larvae pupate within two weeks.

Adults:

Normally seen flying in open fields and gardens.

Interesting facts:

Monarchs (found west of the Rockies) overwinter in southwestern California and migrate to the Northwest during the spring. Eastern monarchs overwinter in Mexico and migrate in the spring to the North (as far as the Great Lakes). What a distance for such a small insect! In the Southeast, thousands of monarch butterflies can be seen flying south to their overwintering grounds in Mexico.

Once in Mexico, the adults congregate on trees in such large numbers that they obscure the vegetation. Monarch butterflies mate in Mexico. Then, when temperatures get warmer in the northern regions, they begin their flight back to the North. Adults typically do not make it back all the way to the northern areas in the U.S. Females lay their eggs on milkweed plants in the southeast and this next generation continues the migration to the north. I wonder how the new generation of monarch butterflies learn to continue northwards? Why do you think monarch butterflies migrate every year? Hint: where is the abundance of milkweed plants in the northern areas of the U.S. during the winter?

Unfortunately some monarch butterflies seem to be attracted to the yellow reflectors that are located in the middle of the road. They probably think these reflectors are flowers. As a result, some of the butterflies are hit by cars, usually getting stuck in the grill. Notoriously, monarch butterflies are unpalatable to most species of birds. But did you know that some grosbeaks and orioles in Mexico eat them? Grosbeaks seem to be immune to monarch toxins and gobble them up. Orioles have a more unique way of eating them: they slice open monarch abdomens and eat only the insides, leaving the skins that contain most of the toxins.

For years, the viceroy butterfly (*Basilarchia archippus*) was thought to be a tasty treat for birds because it mimics the distasteful monarch to escape predation. Researchers have now shown that the viceroy is also repellent to most birds. Thus, viceroys are also using bright warning colorations to let birds know that they are yucky!

· CADDISFLIES ·

ORDER: TRICHOPTERA

A lthough not many people know the winged adults on sight, many people have observed caddisfly larvae in streams and ponds. They construct cases made of small pebbles, sand, and twigs, which are held together with silk or cemented with saliva from the larvae. Each species builds a uniquely shaped case. Some species even build funnel-like nets in streams to trap vegetation and small aquatic organisms that are floating downstream (kind of like spider webs). You can find the cases of aquatic caddisfly larvae under stones, fallen branches, and in crevices at the bottom of streams. They are really interesting to see; take a look sometimes.

Adult caddisflies are rather mothlike and are found swarming over the surface of water at dusk. Dull colored, they are also clumsy fliers.

Natural Life History of Caddisflies

Depending on the species, adults live between four and twenty days and range in size from 1.5 to 25 mm. They are known to sip flower nectar and are normally nocturnal. Males swarm to attract females, and after females fly through a swarm, coupled pairs fall to the vegetation below to complete the mating ritual.

Females normally climb underwater to deposit their eggs in small, gelatinous clumps under sticks and leaves in fresh water, or the eggs are deposited on the surface of the water, after which they sink down to the sludge near the bottom. Most females die soon after oviposition.

Larvae are aquatic and many species build cases out of various debris; the larvae will remain in the cases even while moving about. What is the importance of building a case? Caddisfly larvae pupate inside the case and when they are ready to emerge as adults, the pupae swim to the surface and complete the final molt. Most species emerge as adults at night. Why do you suppose that is?

We should challenge the caddisflies to a clumsy flying contest!

Fun Things to Do with Caddisflies

It is very interesting to raise caddisfly larvae in an aquarium because of the intricately designed cases they construct and carry around on their backs, much like hermit crabs. Here are some interesting questions you can answer. When do larvae construct cases? Do they repair the cases often? If you remove a larvae from a case, what happens?

You can trap adults near ponds or streams by turning on a light at night (they are attracted to light). Place a bunch of adults in a net covered aquarium and watch them mate and lay eggs. How does the female lay eggs? What do they look like?

Common Caddisflies Hit by Cars and Trucks

☐ COMMON CADDISFLIES (Order: Trichoptera)

Local distribution:

These insects are encountered on most roads at night in the spring, summer, and fall.

Eggs and larvae:

Eggs and larvae are found in various streams and ponds. Larvae construct cases.

Adults:

Adults are dull-colored winged individuals.

· CICADAS ·

ORDER: HOMOPTERA
FAMILY: CICADIDAE

Cicadas produce an abnormally loud, continuous sound during most of the summer months. Sometimes it can be quite deafening when you are walking by a cluster of trees. To me, this sound means summer is here. It is produced by males during the day, serenading any females that happen to be close by. Males "sing" by vibrating a pair of drum-like organs located in the thorax, directly behind the head.

Singing cicadas are frequently found in mythology and folklore. For example, one of Aesop's fables talks about how cicadas were once men. In this fable, some people loved to sing and play instruments so much that they forgot about eating and drinking. Eventually, these people died and were transformed into cicadas that seemingly require no food or drink, but sing away until they die.

Each cicada produces a characteristic "squawk" when captured or disturbed. Have you ever caught a cicada? The first time I grabbed one, it squawked, and I instantly released it. However, there is no need to worry, they cannot bite you. The squawk is a defense mechanism to make you leave it alone (which worked on me).

People in the Northeast have heard of the seventeen-year cicada that appears in huge numbers every seventeen years. Other species with shorter life cycles (i.e., 4 to 8 years) are found all over the U.S. Broods overlap so that adults appear every year. Altogether, 166 species of cicadas occur in the U.S. One species, *Neocicada hieroglyphica*, comes out in early April. It is so named because the markings on its back resemble Egyptian hieroglyphics. A larger species in the genus *Tibicen*, nicknamed dog-day cicadas, appears in July and August. Dog-day cicadas are called this because they come out during the hottest period of the summer—I guess when dogs are frequently seen panting.

Natural Life History of Cicadas

Cicadas lay eggs, which are long, white and narrow, in the stems of trees and bushes. The act of embedding the eggs into the stems leaves large marks with frayed wood fibers around the opening.

The eggs hatch in about a month, and the nymphs (larvae) drop to the ground and bury themselves in the soil, feeding on the roots of plants. Larvae construct a hollow ball around themselves, and continually pack down the insides of this cell. Even when moving, larvae will continually remake this cell. (Why do you think they do this?) When a nymph is ready to molt into an adult, it crawls up the nearest tree and attaches itself to the bark. Adult cicadas live for a month or so, depending on the species. Presumably adult cicadas feed upon the sap of trees, but nobody really knows for sure. (Anybody want to investigate?)

Fun Things to Do With Cicadas

Collecting cicadas is fun, but difficult. The adults are located high up in trees and will fly away from your grasp when disturbed. The easiest way to trap adults is to catch them when they have just emerged from the ground. To do this, first find a tree with lots of cicada shells on the ground. These shells are shed by the larvae when they become adults. Once located, get up early in the morning (before 8 AM), and you may find a few nymphs on the trunk that are breaking out of their shells. When they first emerge, they are slow and easy to catch.

Place a few adults in a cage and observe them. How do they sing? Can you tell the difference between a male and female? Do they sing in colder temperatures? What does the male do when a female gets close? Do males sing more with females around? Provide some branches from where you found the cicadas. How do they eat? When do they eat? What do they eat? Do they even eat?

The enterprising person can solve the mystery of how long the larval stage is and how many times cicada nymphs molt. This would be a most interesting and informative project! Obtain some twigs with eggs and wait for them to hatch out. Provide some soil at the bottom of the cage and feed the larvae a variety of plant roots (e.g., grasses). Which roots do larvae prefer? This project may take four to six years, but I bet entomologists would be interested in the results!

Common Cicadas Hit by Cars and Trucks

☐ **DOG-DAY CICADAS (*Tibicen canicurlaris*)**

Local distribution:

These insects are encountered on most roads in the north- and southeastern U.S., as well as Texas, Colorado, Kansas, and Montana during the day from July to August.

Eggs and nymphs:

Eggs are deposited in the stems of trees. Nymphs stay underground and feed on roots.

Adults:

These cicadas are abundant in July and August.

Interesting facts:

The body length of adults can be as large as 41 mm. Their coloration is usually a greenish-brown.

☐ **SOUTHWESTERN CICADA (*Tibicen resh*)**

Local distribution:

These cicadas are encountered on most roads in the southwestern and central U. S. during the day in the summer.

Eggs and nymphs:

Eggs are deposited in stems of trees. Nymphs are underground and feed on roots.

Adults:

These cicadas are common during the summer, and I found quite a few adults located on Palo Verde trees in Arizona.

☐ **NEOCICADAS (*Neocicada hieroglyphica hieroglyphica*)**

Local distribution:

These insects are encountered on most roads in the north- and southeastern U.S., as well as Kansas and Montana during the day from April through August.

Eggs and nymphs:

Eggs are deposited in dead oak tree twigs. Nymphs stay underground and feed on roots.

Adults:

Neocicadas are the dominant species in April, June, and the beginning of July.

Interesting facts:

These cicadas are recognizable because they have dark, squiggly lines on the thorax (resembling Egyptian hieroglyphics, hence their name). The adults, approximately 22 to 25 cm long, are much smaller than dog-day cicadas.

· COCKROACHES ·

ORDER: DICTYOPTERA

O h, Nelly . . . these are the most hated pests in homes throughout the country, and yes (in case you were wondering) several species actually do fly! I do not know of another insect that strikes such fear and repulsion in the hearts of most human beings. People have long associated cockroaches with poor hygiene; however, because many parts of the U.S. are relatively warm year-round, every home owner has these most unwanted critters in their homes. With a continual inflow of cockroaches from outdoor sources, even the best of houses cannot escape their presence.

In fact, did you know that cockroaches prefer better built houses, even though they may be "cleaner" then rundown houses? Cockroaches are sensitive to air flow and prefer less drafty houses. Newer houses, which are built to prevent drafts, can attract a large pest population whereas older houses can be relatively pest free! The next time you see a cockroach in your house, you can claim with pride that your house is soundly built! Well, don't be too boastful. The most important factors that determine the number of cockroaches in your home are moisture and food. The more sources of water and food there are in your home, the larger the population of cockroaches you will have.

Cockroaches are ancient insects and have been relatively unchanged (in appearance) since the Carboniferous period 350 million years ago when they were the most abundant winged insect. Huh! Imagine that! Modern-day cockroaches closely resemble 350 million-year-old cockroaches! Worldwide, over 3,500 species of cockroaches have been identified, and a majority of them occur in the tropics, dwelling in and around forests and jungles. In fact, fewer than one percent of the 3,500 species inhabit human domiciles. For example, in the state of Florida, there are approximately thirty-three species of cockroaches (sixty-nine in the United States), but only five or six species are closely associated with human households. Most species are never seen by humans!

Although a majority of cockroaches live outdoors, long ago a few species gained access to human shelters and their associated food supplies, and they've been cohabiting with humans ever since. In North America, two of the most recognized domestic species are the big, reddish-brown American cockroach and the small, tan German cockroach. Despite their names, both species are believed to be natives of North Africa, and researchers hypothesize they were first introduced to the Americas during early commerce between the two continents.

Surprisingly, most domesticated cockroaches in North America were imported from overseas. These cockroaches, being relatively small, difficult to see, nocturnal, and very crafty, hitched rides on ships and followed humans around the world. Cockroaches were quite happy to abide in areas of the ship considered "disgusting" by humans.

Because of their habits, cockroaches are potential carriers of disease (e.g., Salmonella). Although it is known that they can carry diseases, it is not known whether cockroaches significantly transmit certain diseases to humans. To be on the safe side, I certainly would not eat food that had been contaminated by cockroaches. Furthermore, many people are allergic to cockroaches. "House dust," a familiar allergen, contains cockroach cuticles and feces, which cause allergic reactions in many people.

Overall, you should not fear cockroaches. They cannot bite, and although they look and feel icky, they are basically harmless and will always be a familiar sight in households (especially in the Southeast). I wonder where people acquire such an extreme fear of cockroaches? Sure, they hang out in dirty habitats, but cockroaches are really clean animals. If you ever observe a cockroach for any extended period of time, you will notice they groom themselves quite frequently. (Why do you suppose they groom?).

They are also rather unique organisms. First of all, several species have become resistant to a wide variety of pesticides (notably German cockroaches) and are continually one step ahead of the pesticide industry. Also, they are found worldwide in almost every human habitat (even in Alaska!). Cockroaches have a variety of ways of producing an abundance of young cockroaches (called nymphs). Some species carry eggs around in a hard, oval capsule (an "ootheca," pronounced oh-oh, thee-kuh) until they hatch, whereas others deposit the ootheca right away in a safe spot.

Cockroaches also have a wide range of defenses against predators. Various species have an uncanny way of escaping into small cracks and crevices, and others can spray a most repellent odor when alarmed (e.g., *Eurycotis floridana*—sometimes called the "palmetto bug").

You may think I'm crazy to have such a fascination for cockroaches. I am partial to them since I did my thesis on German cockroaches at the University of Florida. They are truly adaptable critters!

They are kinda cute ... (kinda)

Natural Life History of Cockroaches

Most cockroaches are nocturnal, coming out at night to feed and scurry around. Adults (as well as nymphs) are sensitive to UV light and seem to respond primarily to vibrations and air currents. (Tiptoe into your kitchen one night and quietly turn on the light—do the cockroaches immediately run away?) Cockroaches are actually quite social. Adults release an aggregation pheromone, found in the feces, that cause others to slow down and gather in one particular area. Imagine, if you can, humans gathering together under the same circumstances. What a sight that would be!

Males actively court females; in fact, they entice females with their own version of candy. For example, German and American male cockroaches lift their hindwings to expose an oily secretion that attracts females. Females climb on top of males to feed on this nutritious love potion, and in the meantime, males slide underneath to copulate with the females.

In human domiciles, cockroaches reproduce year-round. Females produce oothecae within eight to fifteen days after reaching the adult stage. On average, twenty-eight German cockroach nymphs or twelve American cockroach nymphs hatch from each ootheca. German cockroaches carry the oothecae until the nymphs emerge, whereas American cockroaches glue oothecae to surfaces as soon as the oothecae are formed. (What are the pluses and minuses of each strategy?) It takes about two months for German nymphs to develop into adults whereas American development takes six months (five to seven molts for both species). When a cockroach molts, the emerging body is entirely white, turning dark in an hour.

Regarding the control of cockroaches, people usually pick up the phone and call the nearest pest control company at the sight of one or two of them. Although pest control operators are normally efficient in getting rid of the ones inside the home, many outdoor cockroaches will infiltrate your house in the near future, and you will have a new population in a few months. Additionally, even though the pesticides used today are normally safe if applied under strict directions, many people do not like the smell or the thought of pesticides in their homes.

Here are a few home remedies. You can make a bait out of dough and boric acid (which is basically nontoxic to humans) by mixing ¼ cup of boric acid (available at a pharmacy), ¼ cup of sugar, and ½ cup of flour. Add water until it is doughy. Put small balls of the mixture in bottle caps and place them in areas that cockroaches frequent. I also recommend trying an alternate method: mix ¼ cup of boric acid, ¼ cup of sugar, and 1 cup of water. Place this liquid mixture into small vials (i.e., film containers), and stop up the entrance with one or two cotton balls. The cotton balls must be damp, but no liquid should seep through when the vial is turned upside down. It would be interesting to see which method works best.

How about a more biological method? Geckos (small lizards), which hang out on the outside walls of your house, love to eat cockroach nymphs. Catch a few geckos (be careful because their tails will fall off if you grab them too hard), and place them in your kitchen, bathroom, or anywhere a cockroach problem exists. They are nocturnal so they will not be seen during the day (they will hide almost anywhere), and actually, they are quite cute! If your geckos are happy, you might hear them call softly to each other during the night (rrrhh! rrrhh! rrrhh!).

The most effective way to reduce the number of cockroaches is to remove potential food and water sources. Cockroaches love to get into open garbage cans, under leaky water pipes, and into food-stuff left on the kitchen counter.

Fun Things to Do with Cockroaches

There are at least six different kinds of cockroaches that can be caught easily with a quart-size can. For bait, place a piece of bread soaked with beer (or any type of sweet drink, if one prefers) inside the can. Make sure you apply a thin layer of Vaseline or mineral oil to the top 1 to 2 inches of the can, so the roach cannot escape once entering. In the evening, place the can near an opening where you think cockroaches hide; the next morning, check the can and you most likely will have several cockroaches.

The best places to catch outdoor cockroaches (usually Smokybrown, Australian, American, and Wood cockroaches) are near knotholes in large live oak trees or in the trunks of palm trees. Try setting the traps on different trees, to see what trees cockroaches prefer and why. Focus on the different microhabitats in each of the trees (e.g., on the trunk, out on limbs, and down by the roots). You can find some species of cockroaches in the thick, vegetative mats that occur on the limbs of oak trees.

You can keep a few cockroaches in a ten gallon aquarium with the sides greased to prevent escapes. Watch their mating behavior—what do the males do when females pass by? Females of most domestic species are generally wider and fatter than males. You can readily initiate mating behavior if you separate males and females for about a week, and then place them in the same container. As you will soon see, males of several species will raise their wings in the presence of a female. What is it about the female that makes the male dance? Is it the odor or the actual presence of the female? You can design a few ingenious experiments to test this. For example, you can collect the "smell" of females by placing a piece of paper in a cage full of females. After a day or so, transport this paper into a cage of males and watch what happens. Try and present a female to males without allowing the males to "smell" her. Do the males respond?

You can also compare indoor (usually German and American cockroaches) to outdoor varieties. Focus on how different species respond to light and vibration. How fast do they scurry away from you? Also note the size, color, smell, and any antipredator defenses. For instance, the *Eurycotis* cockroach sprays a compound that smells like almonds. Be careful! Do not hold these cockroaches up close to your face or they might spray you!

See if you can answer these questions regarding indoor cockroaches: why are they living in human households? How do humans and their domiciles benefit the cockroach? Why don't all insects live inside human households?

You can also test what attracts cockroaches (e.g., different foods); you might discover a new bait! How do cockroaches smell their food? What makes them run? Test their response to light and air currents. What part of the cockroach detects light and air currents? Why do they only come out at night?

Sprinkle some corn flour on a cockroach and watch what it does. It will probably start grooming right away (even a cockroach keeps itself clean!). What part does it groom first and with what? Why groom?

Common Cockroaches Hit by Cars and Trucks

☐ THE ASIAN COCKROACH (*Blattella asahinia*)

Local distribution:

The cockroach is currently encountered on roads in Central Florida at night.

Eggs and nymphs:

Each ootheca (egg case) contains about forty eggs, and they are retained by the female until they hatch. The nymphs reach the adult stage in about six to seven weeks.

Adults:

Adults look just like German cockroaches; they are small (10 to 15 mm long) and tan with two discrete dark parallel bands behind the head.

Interesting facts:

This cockroach is a recent invader of Florida, having been introduced in 1984 from Asia. It is currently found in central Florida; several populations have been found in Lakeland (Polk County) and near Tampa (Hillsborough County). It is thought that in the near future this species will soon be found in all parts of Florida and throughout the Southeast.

The Asian cockroach is similar to the German cockroach, except it can fly and can live outdoors. It is also attracted to brightly lit surfaces and once inside a home, it is known to crawl on illuminated TV sets.

☐ THE AMERICAN COCKROACH (*Periplaneta americana*)

Local distribution:

This cockroach is encountered on all roads at night, but primarily on warm nights in the South after a heavy rain.

Eggs and nymphs:

Each ootheca contains about thirteen eggs and are deposited soon after formation. Nymphs reach the adult stage in about six months.

Adults:

The adults are large (28 to 24 mm long) and red-brown with a pale yellow area behind the head.

Interesting facts:

This cockroach is sometimes called a "palmetto bug" because it is large and hangs out in palmettos and palm trees. However, almost any big, dark insect is called a palmetto bug. In fact, several species of cockroaches are found in palm trees, including Australian, Smokybrown, and *Eurycotis*. American cockroaches can fly and frequently migrate after a summer rain.

· CRANE FLIES ·

ORDER: DIPTERA
FAMILY: TIPULIDAE

Many people have mistaken crane flies for huge mosquitoes. These insects are rather slender, and although they cannot bite, a typical reaction of people to one is, "Aauugghh!"

There are approximately 1,500 North American crane fly species, and they live in aquatic environments or in considerably damp areas. Overall, the natural life history of these delicate creatures is poorly understood.

Natural Life History of Crane Flies

The life span of an adult crane fly is only a few days, and most of it is spent on reproduction. Males of larger species usually congregate around females emerging from the pupae stage. Some species will mate with a female even before her shell has had a chance to harden! Males of smaller species will swarm and latch onto females that have entered into a mass of flying males. Adults are thought not to feed (they just survive long enough to mate), but some species may feed on the nectar of plants. Here is an interesting question: Why do males swarm?

Although the time spent as an adult is short, crane fly larvae live quite a bit longer (up to several months in some species). The larvae of crane flies can be found in moss, damp grass, mud, decaying wood, and aquatic habitats. Aquatic larvae are air breathers and can remain submerged for only a short period of time. Some aquatic larvae are predators and eat dragonfly nymphs, fly larvae, and even members of their own species!

Fun Things to Do with Crane Flies

Crane flies have not been studied by many people, so almost anything you do will be novel. A fun activity would be to determine the number of different species in your neighborhood. If you live near a pond or stream, capture a few of the larvae and raise them at home (take a look in an entomology book to determine what the crane fly larvae look like). You can capture larvae by scooping the bottom of a water reservoir with a bucket or overturning a decaying log.

Place aquatic crane fly larvae in an aquarium and watch them grow. How do they catch prey and what do they eat? Most likely, the larvae will eat decaying organic matter and small insects. How long does it take for the larvae to become adults? If you allow the adults to emerge and mate, you can observe the type of eggs they lay and how they lay them. It would be interesting to know whether some of the predaceous larvae eat mosquito larvae. Find a few mosquito larvae and place them next to a crane fly larvae. Does it eat the mosquito larvae? Maybe you could find a crane fly that could help control mosquito populations!

Common Crane Flies Hit by Cars and Trucks

☐ **CRANE FLIES (Family: Tipulidae)**

Local distribution:

Crane flies are encountered on all roads that are situated near dense vegetation or water. They are active at night and during the day, especially in the spring and summer.

Eggs and larvae:

Eggs and larvae are found in moist or aquatic environments.

Adults:

The adults can be quite large (20 to 80 mm).

· CUCUMBER BEETLES ·

ORDER: COLEOPTERA
FAMILY: CHRYSOMELIDAE
GENUS: DIABROTICA

Farmers and gardeners are quite familiar with cucumber beetles because they are pests to agriculture crops, such as corn, sweet potatoes, cucumbers, peanuts, and beans. Several species, commonly called corn rootworms, are found in the North and West. Larvae feed on the roots of corn plants, and adults feed on the silk, preventing fertilization and subsequent kernel development. Corn damage from these pests have cost farmers in the United States as much as one billion dollars per year!

In the Southeast, the spotted cucumber beetle (*Diabrotica undecimpunctata howardi*), sometimes called the southern corn rootworm, or the banded cucumber beetle (*Diabrotica balteata*) are common pests of cucumber, squash, beans, and corn.

Beetles (or Coleopterans) are the largest order of insects with over 250,000 known species, 30,000 occurring in the United States. You can distinguish beetles from other insects by observing the wings. All beetles have a front pair of thick, mostly hard wings that meet in a straight line down the middle of the back. These front wings cover a membranous pair of hind wings that are folded up underneath.

When you see a straight line down the middle of two thick, hard wings of an insect. . . it's a beetle!

Natural Life History of Cucumber Beetles

Adults are small (2.5 to 11.0 mm in length), yellow-bodied insects with dark spots or stripes. Adults feed on more than 280 different plants; they tend to prefer the floral parts. Adults live approximately eighty days.

Females produce sex pheromones that attract male cucumber beetles. Adults mate soon after emergence from the pupae stage, and females oviposit within fourteen days. Eggs are oviposited in moist soil, 4 to 5 inches underground, in the roots of host plants. Some females can lay over a thousand eggs. Whew! That's an awful lot of offspring. Good thing these insects are small!

Eggs normally hatch within ten days, and larvae transform into adults twenty-five days later. Larvae feed on the roots and stems of host plants.

Fun Things to Do with Cucumber Beetles

You can find a large number of adults in the silk of small ears of corn in the spring and early summer. Alternatively, you can collect the larvae and pupae by digging up the roots of corn left in corn fields after the harvest. Larvae are small and white.

To raise them at home, build a couple of small cages, and provide plenty of water (soaked cotton balls work best) and host plant material for them to eat. In order to observe some interesting behaviors, I suggest separating males from females. Adult male abdomens have rather blunt ends whereas females are pointed. You can also sex the pupae with the aid of a microscope—females have an extra pair of distinct papillae (they look like small nipples) on the end of their abdomen whereas males do not.

Find out how males recognize females. Place a virgin female (one that has not encountered a male) enclosed in an air-tight vial into a cage of males. Do the males congregate around the vial? Now place a female that is enclosed in a vial with holes into a cage of males. Do the males crawl around the vial? Do they perform any courtship behaviors? What do you think primarily attracts males to females, the sight of a female or her smell? Obtain a female that has already mated and place her in the cage of males. Do the males congregate around the vial? Why or why not?

Take a piece of paper that has been in a cage full of female beetles and place it in a cage with some males. How do the males respond? Why do you think insects produce sex pheromones? Why can't they just locate each other visually?

Common Cucumber Beetles Hit by Cars and Trucks

☐ **COMMON SPOTTED CUCUMBER BEETLES**
  (*Diabrotica undecimpunctata howardi*) and

☐ **BANDED CUCUMBER BEETLES (*Diabrotica balteata*)**

Local distribution:

These insects are encountered on most roads (not in the Northwest) and are most common in the spring and early summer.

Eggs and larvae:

Eggs and the white larvae are found mostly in the roots of host plants (e.g., corn).

Adults:

Adults are common in the summer and spring.

Interesting facts:

The banded cucumber beetle has light bands across the back, whereas the spotted cucumber beetle has dark spots.

· DRAGONFLIES ·
ORDER: ODONATA

T he bright-colored bodies of these insects attract many casual observers. Anybody on the banks of a pond, lake, or river cannot help but notice these insects flying by. Dragonflies will land on almost any surface, including fishing bobbers, canoes, and even one's finger! These insects are efficient predators and will opportunistically capture many different types of prey, including horseflies, mosquitoes, wasps, bees, and biting flies. Dragonflies are truly the "hawks" of the insect world. I have even heard of dragonflies that "patrol" around canoes, snatching up biting flies attracted to people within the canoe. Dragonflies use a sneak attack on flying insects. They fly underneath the unsuspecting prey and dart upwards and snatch them out of the air. Dragonflies have huge, goggle-like eyes which, because they are positioned on top of the head, enable dragonflies to see all around themselves.

Dragonflies are adept at flying and come in all sizes. Fossil records from 230 million years ago indicate that dragonflies used to have wingspans of several feet! But now, dragonflies are not so big; the largest ones in the U.S. are darners, which have a wingspan of approximately 81.2 to 106.3 mm in length. Why don't we have huge dragonflies, like in the past? Although no sure answer exists, avian (bird) predators probably had something to do with limiting the size of dragonflies.

Damselflies (Suborder: Zygoptera) are often mistaken for dragonflies (Suborder: Anisoptera) because they are similar in appearance. The easiest way to tell the difference between the two is to watch how they hold their wings when resting. Damselflies hold their wings together over their backs, whereas dragonflies hold their wings straight out to their sides.

Natural Life History of Dragonflies

About 400 dragonfly species are found in North America. Adults are normally seen near bodies of water, flying back and forth in seemingly random fashion . . . but if you watch closely, each dragonfly will patrol a defined area, which is usually marked by certain objects in the water or along the shore. All of these dragonflies are males patrolling their territory. They will defend this area against all other males. Sometimes males will display to each other, flexing their brightly colored abdomens (like manly men), and a high speed chase may follow with one sometimes falling into the water.

Territories are defended by males in order to attract and mate with females. Females fly in from surrounding areas and can be seen "checking out" the available males and territories. Males are more brightly colored than females, and males of some species display these colors to approaching females. When a female signals to a male that she is receptive, the male grasps the back of the female with the tip of his abdomen, and the pair assume a wheel position. Females typically mate with several males and oviposit (lay eggs) in their respective territories.

Once sperm has been transferred, the male actively guards the female while she oviposits in the water. Sometimes the male is attached to the female or he may be hovering close by to ward off any other males. You can tell a female is ovipositing when she flies close to the water, periodically submerging the tip of her abdomen. Females of some species have an ovipositor that contains two knife-like blades that are used to place eggs into the stems of aquatic vegetation.

Eggs are oval and covered with a sticky jelly. Once laid, many eggs are snatched up by fish and other aquatic animals. If not eaten, the eggs normally hatch within ten days, and emerging larvae begin feeding right away. The larval stage is quite long in most dragonfly species, lasting one to two years. Larvae are voracious predators, possessing a unique mouthpart, a so-called "lip-trap," that shoots out in $1/100$ of a second to catch any prey that comes close. Dragonfly larvae eat a wide variety of aquatic organisms, including mosquito larvae and small fish!

Larvae breathe underwater with gills that are located in a most unusual place: the anus. The gills are located in the rectal chamber and water is pumped in and out by abdominal muscles. In fact, the larvae can expel water so forcefully that it is an effective propulsion mechanism to escape predators. The larvae of some dragonflies also form territories underwater and defend them against intruders. When an intruder approaches, both larvae will raise their abdomens and display to each other; sometimes the resident will snap its lip-trap at the intruder. Why do you suppose larvae set up territories and defend them?

When the larvae transform into the adult state, they climb out of the water and attach themselves to an upright stem or twig. After breathing in air, which enlarges the body, the larval skin splits and the adult pushes itself out onto a nearby branch. The newly merged adult is soft and helpless. Many birds and ants attack the dragonfly at this time. It inflates its wings by pumping fluid into them, and it holds its breath until its skin hardens, which usually takes a half an hour.

Fun Things to Do with Dragonflies

Watching the growth of dragonfly larvae can be quite exciting. I strongly suggest setting up an aquarium for the larvae. The larvae are really active and you can watch them hunt, feed, and interact with each other. You can collect the eggs in local ponds or streams. Locate an area where dragonflies are breeding and then search the water for eggs. Deposited eggs of some species leave characteristic track marks in the stems of aquatic plants. To collect larvae, pull up an aquatic plant (roots and all) and transplant everything into your aquarium (dragonfly larvae hang out in the roots of aquatic plants during the day). Wait until night, and then peer in with a flashlight to see how many dragonfly (or damselfly) larvae you have!

Dragonfly larvae are easy to rear in an aerated aquarium. Fill the aquarium with plenty of aquatic vegetation and provide a daily supply of aquatic insects for the larvae to feed on (e.g., mosquito larvae). For some species, you should add a layer of sand at the bottom for the larvae to burrow into. Be sure to place some sticks that appear above the water line just in case the larvae are ready to emerge as adults. Over the top of the aquarium, place a large see-through top with plenty of room for the adults to fly around. You can build the frame for this top with fine wire or balsa wood. Glue fine nylon netting onto the frame. (Netting can be found at any fabric store.)

Do some experiments with the larvae. Provide them with different kinds of food items. Which kind do they like best? How do they stalk their prey? Do they sit and wait or do they search through the vegetation? What are the advantages and disadvantages of each strategy? Do they set up territories and how do they defend them? Are they more active during the day or night?

With adults, observations in the wild can be very interesting. When you watch adult dragonflies flying about their territories, you can actually draw a map outlining each territory. How many females oviposit in each territory? How many aggressive interactions occur between males? Make a few models of male dragonflies and dangle them over a territory with a fishing pole. What colors and motions of the model do males respond to? Remove an individual from its territory. How long does it take for a new dragonfly to take over?

To catch an adult, use a butterfly net and approach the dragonfly from the back end. Once in the net, hold the wings together above the back and slowly remove him from the net. Be careful! Try and prevent the dragonfly from clamping down on the net with its jaws; sometimes you will accidentally pull its head right off! Place the dragonfly in a large envelope with its wings and abdomen stretched out flat. If the abdomen is curled, a dragonfly may bite off a portion of it. Label the flap of the envelope with information about when and where you caught the dragonfly. If you want to mark an individual, you can place a dot on the wing with a waterproof pen.

Place an adult in a cage, throw in a few flies, and watch an amazing predator hunt. How do they catch and eat the flies? Dragonflies have enormous eyes—why do you think they have large eyes? Watch its head. It moves very quickly!

If you want to preserve a specimen, first kill the dragonfly by placing an envelope (containing the dragonfly) in a bottle of acetone for a few seconds. Be careful, acetone is flammable and should not be inhaled. Then remove the envelope, extract the dragonfly and spread its wings out flat, abdomen straight. Then, soak it in acetone again for twenty-four hours. This process preserves the colors and kills bacteria that decompose the body. You can also freeze dragonflies in your freezer.

If you have questions about dragonflies, write the International Odonata Research Institutes, P.O. Box 1269, Gainesville, FL 32602-1269.

Common Dragonflies Hit by Cars and Trucks

☐ THE COMMON GREEN DARNER (*Anax junius*)

Local distribution:

These insects are encountered on most roads during the spring, summer, and fall, especially on roads located near water.

Eggs and larvae:

Eggs are oviposited by the female in submerged and floating aquatic plants.

Adults:

Males are usually seen flying low during the day patrolling territories. Males have a green thorax and blue abdomen, whereas females have a green thorax and brownish-green abdomen.

Interesting facts:

These dragonflies are large (68 to 84 mm long). Green darners are known to eat wasps, butterflies, moths, and flies. They have been reported to have attacked hummingbirds! This is one of the few species in which the male holds onto the female while she is laying eggs.

☐ SKIMMERS (Family: Libellulidae)

Local distribution:

Skimmers are encountered on most roads during the spring, summer, and fall, especially those roads located near water.

Eggs and larva:

Eggs are oviposited in the water or on the bank.

Adults:

These dragonflies are the dominant species in ponds.

Interesting facts:

Females of some species (e.g., king skimmers) gather drops of water, release a few eggs into the droplets, and throw the drops of water onto the bank. Why do you think they do this? Other females dip their abdomen into the water, releasing the eggs. One species, the eastern pondhawk (*Erythemis simplicicollis*), is cannibalistic. It is a ferocious dragonfly and will attack large horseflies. Place a few of these dragonflies near a horse stable and watch the subsequent aerial dogfight! You will cheer for each biting fly taken by these formidable hunters!

· Fireflies ·

Order: Coleoptera
Family: Lampyridae

lthough called fireflies, these insects are not true flies (order: Diptera) but actually beetles. Everyone, from kids to adults, is fascinated by fireflies because they produce light. Kids spend many a summer night trying to catch these luminescent insects, placing them in jars to make "bug lanterns." The production of light by animals is called bioluminescence and although fireflies are the best known insect to produce light, many other animals are bioluminescent, including fish, centipedes, gnats, and worms.

But how do they do it? Fireflies possess a well developed organ on the ventral (lower) side of the abdomen that consists of a layer of light-producing cells, behind which another layer of cells reflects the light out. The light is produced by a complex reaction (in the presence of oxygen) that oxidizes a substance called luciferin. Fireflies apparently control this reaction by regulating the amount of oxygen entering the light-producing organ. What is unique about this light reaction is that no heat is given off! Have you ever touched an electric light bulb? It is really hot because most of the energy released is heat, not light. However, a firefly's rear end never gets hot because the only energy given off is light!

Why do fireflies produce light? Fireflies use light flashes for mating purposes. Males and females flash to each other in a specific sequence to locate each other to reproduce. In many American fireflies, males fly around broadcasting a species-specific signal to which females, located on the ground, respond by flashing a signal to let the male know where she is. However, several female fireflies (genus *Photuris*) will mimic the mating signal of other firefly species and eat the unlucky males that land next to them. Can you imagine their surprise?

Natural Life History of Fireflies

Adult males fly about emitting flashes just after sunset; females, located in the vegetation below, respond to the males overhead by flashing their own signal. After seeing a flashing female, a male will fly down to her and crawl around the vegetation until he locates her. The couple immediately copulate and remain together for about twelve to seventy-two hours, depending on the species. Both sexes normally do not feed, but rely upon energy reserves from previous larval stages.

Females lay their eggs approximately two days after mating in various locations, including aquatic vegetation, moist leaf litter, and moist soil among plant roots. Eggs are laid in small batches, totaling up to one hundred eggs.

Eggs normally glow in the dark and hatch within two weeks. Larvae are predators, feeding on snails, worms, and possibly small caterpillars. Larvae are active mainly at night and also glow. Larvae pupate in about sixty days and emerge as adults approximately one week after pupating.

Fun Things to Do with Fireflies

These insects are really fun to catch . . . watch for their flashing abdomens! Four green spots on the lower abdomen cause the firefly to light up. Male fireflies can be caught flying in the air, whereas females can be caught in the vegetation. Males are 7 to 11 mm long and females are 9 to 10 mm long. Further, females are heavier and have smaller light organs than males.

You can collect larvae by looking in the vegetation for small, "crawly" things that glow in the dark. Also, some larvae can be found among aquatic vegetation (e.g., cattails and water hyacinths) in most ponds during the summer.

Set up a few cages for the larvae and/or adults. Firefly larvae will eat snails, worms, and other cut-up insects or caterpillars. If you have a few adults, place the males and females into separate cages. After a few days, put a male into the cage containing the females and observe what happens. When does the male start signaling? The female? How quickly does the male find the female? Does the male always signal the same way? What about the female? You can also watch the courtship and observe where the female deposits the glowing eggs.

Observe the larvae. Do they glow all the time? If not, why do you think they only glow sometimes? Because glowing is obviously not used for mating purposes during the larval stage, why do they glow at all? What happens when you pick a larva up? Does it start glowing right away? How does a larva kill and eat a snail? You will probably discover many unique properties about each species of firefly larvae.

One can also attract adult fireflies by "signaling" to them. In the early evening, go out to any field and carefully observe the flashing patterns of both males and females. (Remember, males are usually signaling while flying and females signal from the vegetation below.) Write down (or videotape) the flashing pattern of a signaling male or female. Be sure to note not only the duration of each flash in sequence, but the length of time between the flashes. You will recognize the start of a flash sequence because there are long pauses between sequences, and each sequence is repeated in exactly the same way.

After determining the flashing pattern of a particular species (pick a species that is relatively abundant in the field), construct your own flashing device. First try a small penlight to imitate firefly flashing patterns. Try to make the light opening as big as the flashing abdomen of a firefly. In the early evening, go out to a field full of fireflies and start signaling! Try imitating a female and see if many male fireflies come down to you. You will be surprised how many fireflies will respond when you signal the correct way! However, you may have to modify your device several times to get a response. For example, try covering the end of your penlight with different colored filters: yellow, green, or red. Which colors do the fireflies respond to the most? Use different types of light bulbs that vary in brightness. You might also want to construct a more sophisticated flashing device with LED lights.

Common Fireflies Hit by Cars and Trucks

☐ COMMON FIREFLIES
(Genera: *Pyractomena, Photuris, Photinus*)

Local distribution:

These insects are encountered on most roads at night throughout the spring/summer.

Eggs and larvae:

Eggs and larvae are found mostly on aquatic vegetation and in moist soil.

Adults:

Adults are common in the spring and summer, recognizable by their flashing abdomens.

Interesting facts:

Photuris species come out all at once in the spring, and the larvae can be found in rotting logs, poorly drained soil, and in forest leaf litter. *Pyractomena* and *Photinus* species can be seen flying near ponds throughout the spring and summer, and the larvae are found underwater on aquatic vegetation.

· GRASSHOPPERS ·

ORDER: ORTHOPTERA
FAMILY: ACRIDIDAE
GENUS: SCHISTOCERA

Grasshoppers in this genus are quite common in meadows and along roadsides in the Southeast. Walking in a meadow, one frequently disturbs a grasshopper and it flies off a short distance. As you attempt to get closer, it flies just out of your reach. If you are fast enough to catch one, it frequently will spit up a dark fluid which stains your fingers and most likely tastes very bitter (although I have never tasted it).

In this genus, there are four species of grasshoppers. The most common and recognizable species is the American grasshopper (*Schistocera americana americana*). It is a large grasshopper (35 to 60 mm long) with black spots on the wings. Interestingly, it is closely related to the desert locust (*Schistocera gregaria*) in Africa that is world-renowned for its ability to swarm and to eat vast amounts of food.

I happened to be in West Africa when the biggest locust outbreak of the past forty years hit. I was a Peace Corps volunteer in Senegal in the fall of 1988. One day, I was out in my village when I noticed what looked like a black cloud coming over the horizon. I soon realized it was locusts, because I had heard previously on the radio that a swarm, flying over the Sahara desert, was about to invade Senegal. I was astounded at the sheer number of insects; the air was thick with them and it was difficult to walk around without being hit. There was a huge green tree in the middle of the village (about as big as a large oak), and I watched in amazement as a small part of the swarm swooped down and devoured every leaf on the tree in fifteen minutes! There were so many locusts on this tree that it appeared red (locusts are red during the swarming phase).

But what I was really unprepared for was when all the eggs that the first swarm had laid, hatched out about three weeks later. The ground was literally covered with little locusts called "hoppers." They ate everything, including each other. In fields with anything green in them, one could hear a general "munching" sound that was actually quite loud. It was even difficult to sleep at night because the baby locusts crawled all around my hut, making an awful racket.

Even more surprising, these locusts caused a number of automobile accidents. So many locusts were run over that their guts made the paved roads really slick, and all cars had to slow down to 40 m.p.h. Riding on my motorcycle was also tricky because locusts kept flying up my helmet. Have you ever tried riding a motorcycle with an insect crawling around the inside of your helmet?

But don't worry, the American grasshopper does not swarm in such vast numbers and is normally not of economic importance. However, there are reported outbreaks that cause considerable damage to citrus crops.

Natural Life History of Grasshoppers

There are normally two generations of grasshoppers each year, one in spring and the other in late summer. A female lays a batch of about eighty-five eggs in the soil, which hatch in one month. The larvae (called nymphs) molt four or five times (over a period of weeks to months) and they may be green, yellow, or orange with black, yellow, or green markings (the colors are quite variable). The larvae have huge appetites and can do considerable damage during this stage. Adult American grasshoppers are a reddish color with black markings.

Fun Things to Do with Grasshoppers

Grasshoppers are common during the summer in relatively dry meadows, and you can either observe them in the wild or catch them with a net. If you want the eggs, observe where the grasshoppers hang out and dig in the soil underneath the vegetation. The surest way, though, is to catch a female full of eggs.

Let's all do the hop!

ANTS

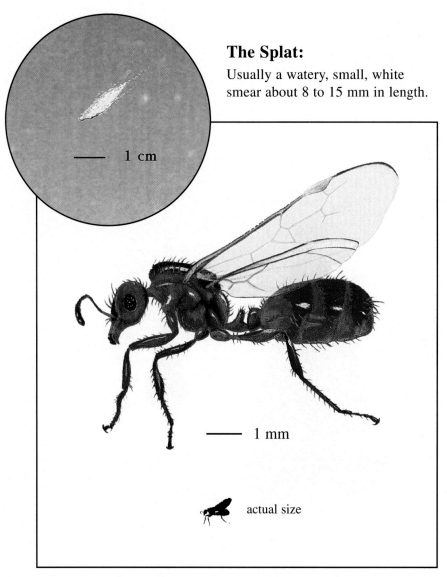

The Splat:
Usually a watery, small, white smear about 8 to 15 mm in length.

—— 1 cm

—— 1 mm

actual size

Illustration: A fire ant (*Solenopsis invicta*).

- PLATE I -

ANTLIONS

The Splat:

Resembles the splat of a flying ant—
a watery, small, white smear about 8
to 15 mm in length.

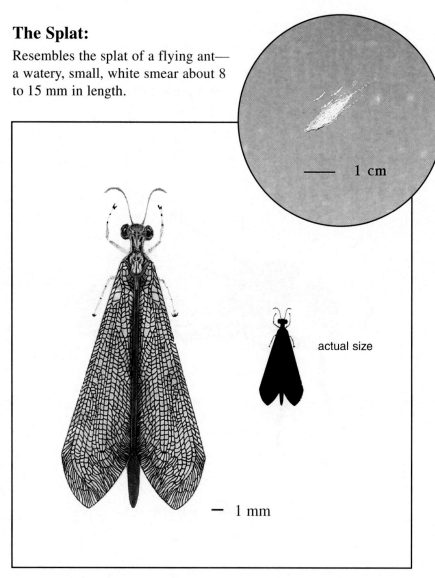

1 cm

actual size

1 mm

Illustration: An adult antlion (*Brachynemurus* spp.).

- PLATE II -

BITING MIDGES
(NO-SEE-UMS)

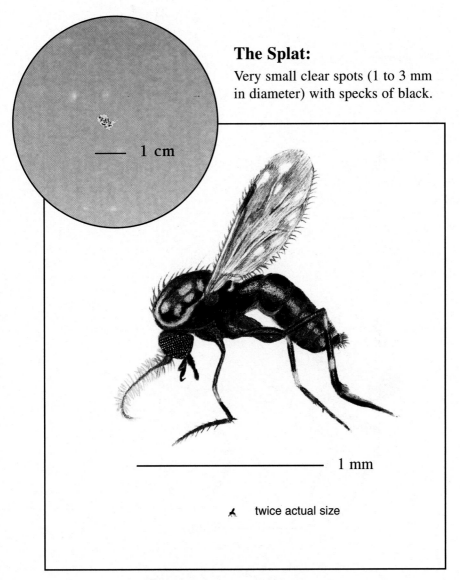

The Splat:
Very small clear spots (1 to 3 mm in diameter) with specks of black.

—— 1 cm

—————————————— 1 mm

twice actual size

Illustration: A typical biting midge
(*Culicoides* [Oecacta] *villos*).

- PLATE III -

BLACK FLIES

The Splat:

Some of these flies leave yellow or
red dots about 3 to 5 mm in diameter.

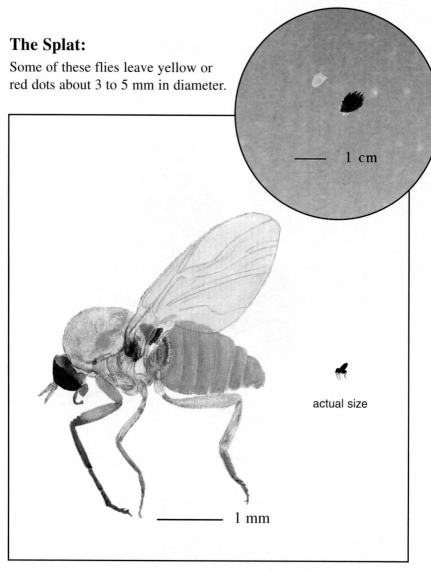

1 cm

actual size

——— 1 mm

Illustration: A typical black fly (*Simulium decoratum*).

- PLATE IV -

BUTTERFLIES AND MOTHS

The Splat:

Butterflies and moths usually leave a thick, gooey, white or yellow substance with lumps in it. The splat is usually strung out from the point of impact (10 to 90 mm), and one can see scales (dust-like particles) scattered around the perimeter.

___ 1 cm

shown at 90% actual size

1 cm

Illustration: A tiger swallowtail butterfly (*Heraclides glaucus*).

- PLATE V -

CADDISFLIES

The Splat:

These insects leave a splat that is spread out with cream-colored edges and a clear center (approximately 10 mm in length).

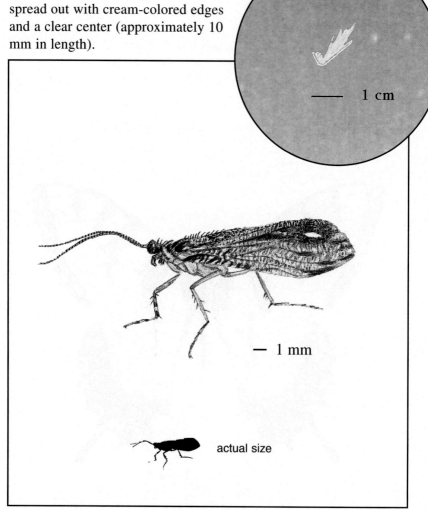

— 1 cm

— 1 mm

actual size

Illustration: A typical caddisfly (*Agrypinia vestita*).

- PLATE VI -

CICADAS

The Splat:

These insects are found on the bumpers and grills of automobiles. Occasionally they will hit the windshield, accompanied by a loud "Whack!" The splat is variable in size (15 to 50 mm in length), whitish in color, and usually contains parts of the insect that are recognizable (e.g., the head).

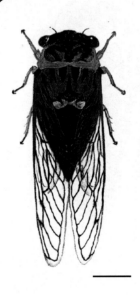

— 1 cm

—— 1 cm

shown slightly larger than actual size

Illustration: A typical cicada (*Tibicen resonans*).

- PLATE VII -

COCKROACHES

The Splat:

Can be a small (3 to 5 mm), white, and oily smear. If you hit a large cockroach (e.g., the American cockroach), the splat is usually quite large (20 to 30 mm), white, and oily with globs of junk stuck in the middle. When you hit one, it produces quite a bang!

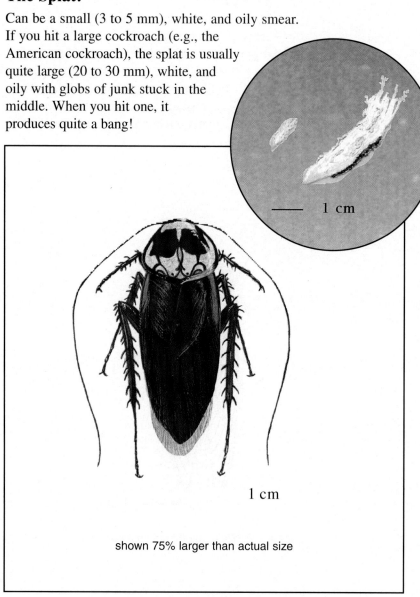

—— 1 cm

1 cm

shown 75% larger than actual size

Illustration: An American cockroach
(*Periplaneta americana*).

- PLATE VIII -

CRANE FLIES

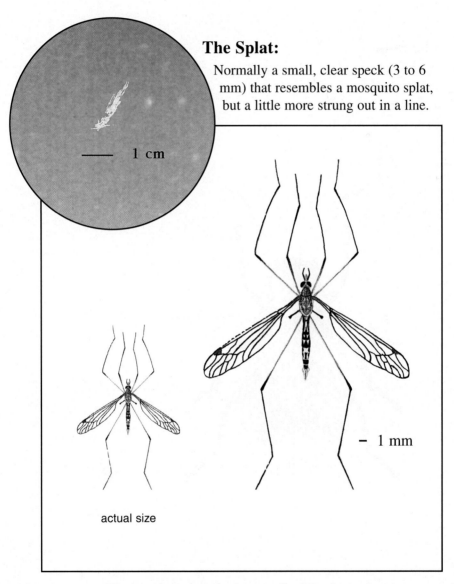

The Splat:

Normally a small, clear speck (3 to 6 mm) that resembles a mosquito splat, but a little more strung out in a line.

1 cm

1 mm

actual size

Illustration: A typical crane fly (*Tipula* spp.).

- PLATE IX -

CUCUMBER BEETLES

The Splat:

Usually a watery, small, yellowish round smear about 5 mm in diameter.

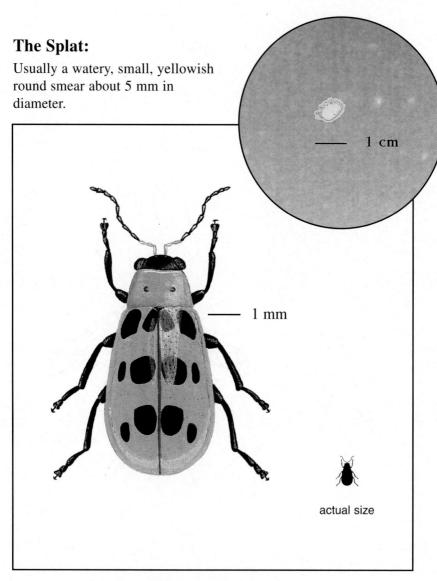

1 cm

1 mm

actual size

Illustration: A spotted cucumber beetle
(*Diabrotica undecimpunctata undecimpunctata*).

- PLATE X -

DRAGONFLIES

The Splat:

Whole dragonflies are usually found on the bumpers and grills of cars where their wings get caught. Occasionally they will hit the windshield, leaving a roundish splat that is variable in length (10 to 30 mm) and transparent-white in color.

—— 1 cm

—— 1 cm

shown slightly larger than actual size

Illustration: A typical dragonfly (*Celithemis eponina*).

- PLATE XI -

FIREFLIES

The Splat:

When fireflies hit the windshield, they usually leave greenish residues (5 to 10 mm in length) that glow for several seconds.

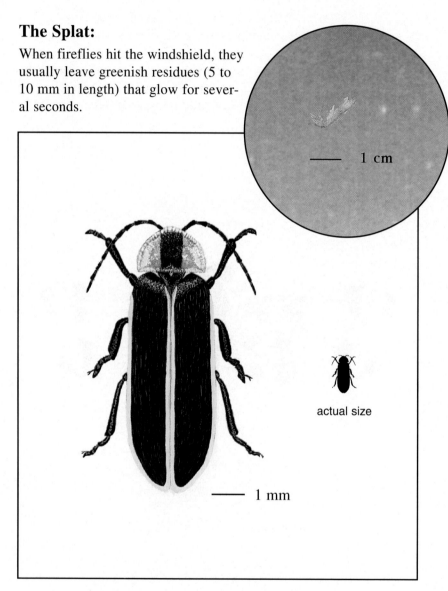

1 cm

1 mm

actual size

Illustration: A typical firefly (*Photinus* spp.).

- PLATE XII -

GRASSHOPPERS

The Splat:

The size of the splat is quite variable (10 to 80 mm in length), but it generally consists of smooth, yellowish-looking gunk.

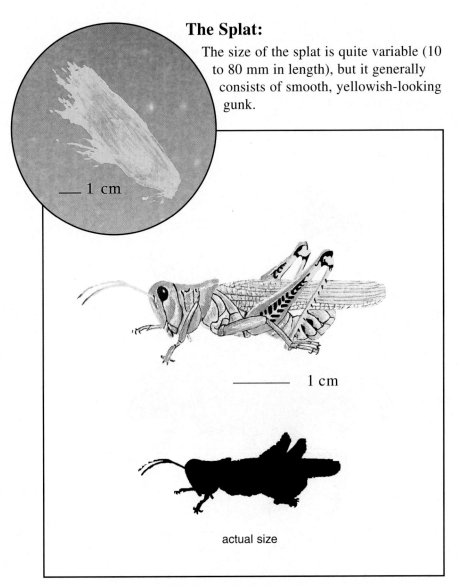

___ 1 cm

_____ 1 cm

actual size

Illustration: A typical American grasshopper (*Melanoplus differentialis*).

- PLATE XIII -

HONEY BEES

The Splat:

A big white round blotch (approximately 10 mm in diameter) with yellow on the edges.

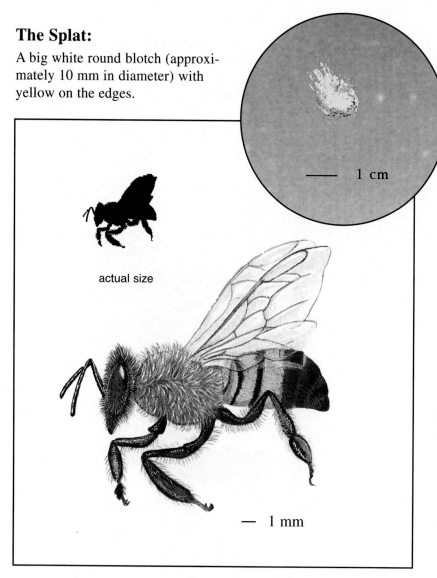

—— 1 cm

actual size

— 1 mm

Illustration: A typical honey bee (*Apis mellifera*).

- PLATE XIV -

HORSE AND DEER FLIES

The Splat:

Usually quite large for horse flies (20 to 70 mm in length) and small for deer flies (8 to 14 mm). Each consists of dirty-white, gooey stuff. There will be a smear of red in it if the fly was full of blood (from an animal).

—— 1 cm

actual size

— 1 mm

Illustration: A typical horse fly (*Tabanus americanus*).

- PLATE XV -

HOVER FLIES

The Splat:

Depending on the size of the hover fly, a splat can be as small as 2 mm and as big as 35 mm. The splat spreads out around the point of impact and usually appears to be yellow and smooth.

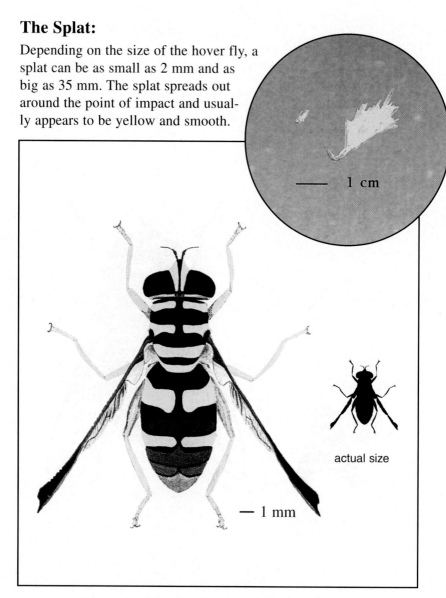

—— 1 cm

—— 1 mm

actual size

Illustration: A hover fly (Family: Syrphidae).

- PLATE XVI -

JUMPING PLANT LICE

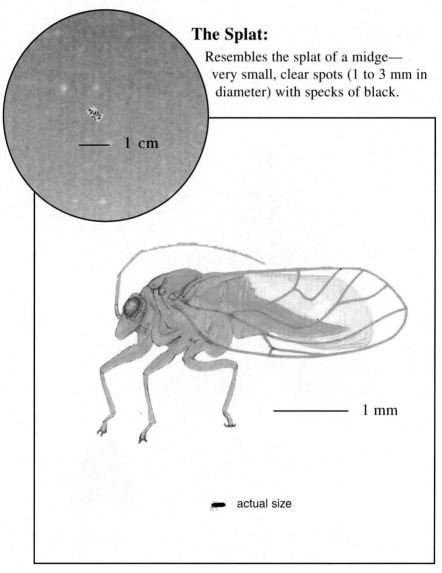

The Splat:

Resembles the splat of a midge—
very small, clear spots (1 to 3 mm in
diameter) with specks of black.

1 cm

1 mm

actual size

Illustration: A typical adult jumping plant louse
(*Psylla carpinicola*).

- PLATE XVII -

Lacewings

The Splat:

Lacewings will always leave a long, thin, greenish line (up to 10 cm in length) with a small blob at one end.

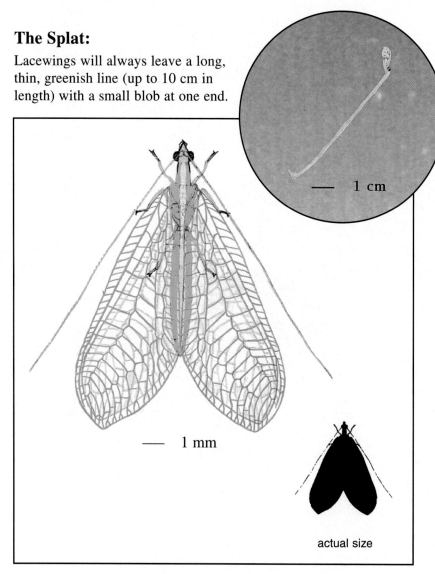

— 1 cm

— 1 mm

actual size

Illustration: A typical green lacewing (*Chrysopa* spp.).

- PLATE XVIII -

LOVEBUGS

The Splat:

Usually clear with small lumps (eggs) near the point of impact. The splat is sprayed upwards (20 to 35 mm in length) and when dry, the splat appears to be creamy or even yellowish in color.

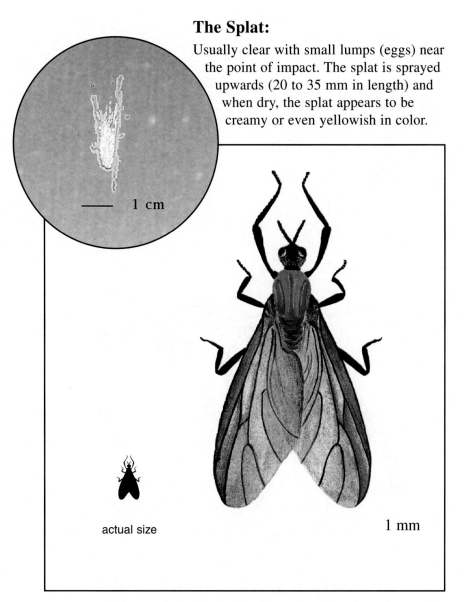

1 cm

actual size

1 mm

Illustration: A typical lovebug (*Plecia* spp.).

- PLATE XIX -

MIDGES

The Splat:

Small, clear spots (2 to 5 mm in
diameter) with specks of black.

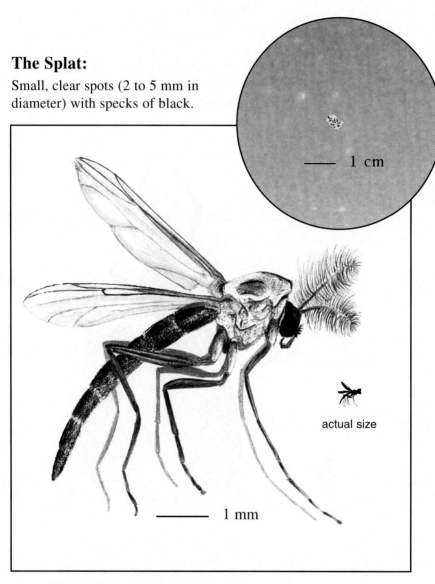

1 cm

1 mm

actual size

Illustration: A typical midge (*Glyptotendipes paripes*).

- PLATE XX -

MOLE CRICKETS

The Splat:

These insects are splattered on the bumpers and grills of automobiles. Occasionally they will hit the windshield, accompanied by a loud "Whack!" The splat is rather large (20 to 30 mm in length), whitish in color, and usually contains parts of the insect that are recognizable (e.g., the head).

1 cm

1 cm

actual size

Illustration: A tawny mole cricket (*Scapteriscus vicinus*).

- PLATE XXI -

Mosquitoes

The Splat:

Normally a small (1 to 2 mm), black-grayish, dry dot. If you hit a female full of blood, the splat will have a touch of red.

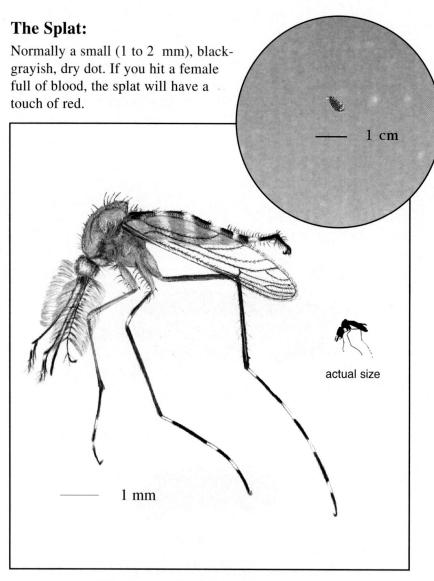

—— 1 cm

—— 1 mm

actual size

Illustration: A typical male mosquito
(*Aedes canadensis*).

- PLATE XXII -

MUSCID FLIES

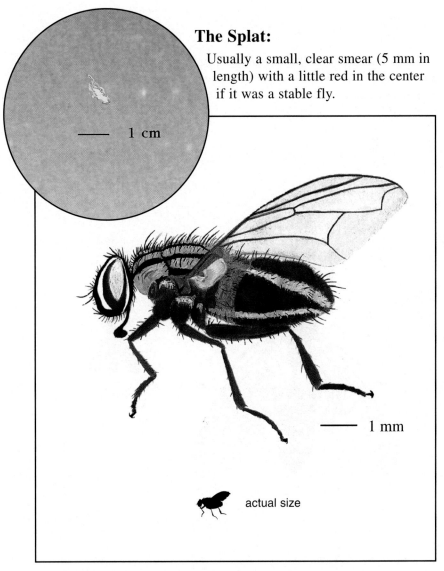

The Splat:

Usually a small, clear smear (5 mm in length) with a little red in the center if it was a stable fly.

—— 1 cm

—— 1 mm

actual size

Illustration: A typical house fly (*Musca domestica*).

- PLATE XXIII -

SOLDIER FLIES

The Splat:

Usually a large, creamy-grey smear
(10 to 30 mm in length) with little
chunks of gunk in the center.

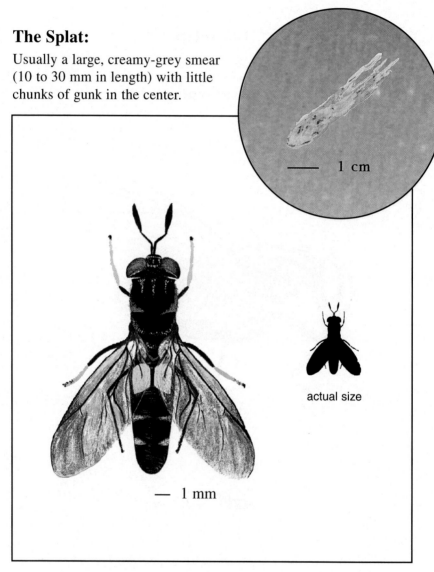

1 cm

actual size

— 1 mm

Illustration: A typical soldier fly (*Hermetia illucens*).

- PLATE XXIV -

Place a few grasshoppers in a covered aquarium and observe their behavior. Do some of the males "sing?" How do they sing? Watch them eat . . . they can really munch!

Common Grasshoppers
Hit by Cars and Trucks

☐ **COMMON GRASSHOPPERS (Genus: *Schistocera*)**

Local distribution:

These insects are on most roads during the day throughout the spring and summer.

Eggs and nymphs:

Eggs are found in the soil of meadows. Nymphs are quite common and come in a variety of colors and sizes.

Adults:

Adults are abundant in the spring and summer.

·Honey Bees·

ORDER: HYMENOPTERA
FAMILY: APIDAE:
GENUS: APIS
SPECIES: MELLIFERA

Busy as a bee ... it is hard not to notice these insects, buzzing from flower to flower during the spring and summer. Humans love honey, which is produced by bees, and there is a long history of people raising bees (beekeeping) for this sweet substance. In fact, Egyptians were beekeepers 4,350 years ago.

Bees are very social and they build large hives in various dry cavities (e.g., tree hollows). Most bees in a colony are female, and one queen lays eggs for the entire colony, sometimes 2,000 eggs a day! Males (drones) are born infrequently, and their sole function is to mate. Females are workaholics—they forage for food, protect the hive, feed the young, and produce honey. Incidentally, did you know that the honey bee in North America was introduced from Europe?

Honey bees have unique ways of communicating with each other; one particular communication ritual, the bee dance, is a way of one bee telling other bees in the colony the location of a good source of food. As humans, we would communicate the location of a specific food resource (i.e., a grocery store) by talking. But bees "dance" a special way to give directions.

Many scientists have studied this dance, but Karl von Frisch from Germany was the first scientist to interpret it. He designed several intricate experiments that showed bees can find the location of a food source from a returning bee by "observing" her dance. This discovery was significant because humans believed that so-called "lower" organisms did not possess complicated communication systems.

While "shaking their booty" seems like an unusual form of behavior, bees have ritualized this behavior to mean something specific. Dancing bees orient their movements in relation to the sun, and they dance at a certain frequency. The angle of the dance indicates the direction of a food source, and the duration of one complete "circuit" of the dance is thought to communicate the distance. Although this dance tells foraging bees the location of a potential food source, departing bees also use a variety of cues, including odor and visual landmarks, to find other feeding patches. Foraging bees use a variety of stimuli to decide in what patch to forage, such as the distance and quality of a food patch, how hungry the hive is, time of day, weather conditions, and obstacles encountered along the way. As an analogous situation, let's say you were given specific directions to a great grocery store several miles away to buy quality peaches. However, on your way, you see (or smell) a peach stand with lower quality peaches only 200 yards away. You may opt to buy the lower quality peaches depending on how hungry you are, what time it is, whether it is rainy or sunny, and how many stoplights there are on the way to the grocery store.

Bees also have another form of communication. They produce odors (called pheromones) to communicate with each other. Honey bees have a variety of odors that elicit numerous responses. For example, queen bees exude a pheromone that prohibits the production of new queens, attracts drones for mating, and tells workers in the hive to take care of the queen. Workers produce a recruitment pheromone that attracts other bees, and they also produce alarm pheromones that make other bees sting when the hive is attacked. Most bees are not that aggressive; it takes a lot to get a bee to sting because once it stings, it dies. The stinger and several internal parts attached to it are left in the victim (some of which help pump toxin into the wound).

This act of sacrificing oneself for the benefit of the hive seems like an unselfish behavior, but actually it is selfish. Why is this so? Well, female bees in the hive are sisters (coming from the one queen) and on average, all female bees share three-quarters of their genes with each other. Now think of a bee as a vehicle for the genes. The genes "know" that exact copies of themselves are housed in other bees in the hive. Thus, from the perspective of the genes residing in a stinging bee, it is selfish to sacrifice the bee to insure the survival of gene copies housed in bees in the rest of the colony. Just a little tidbit to make you go "Hmmmm!"

But why do bees make honey? Certainly it is not just for our enjoyment. Nectar gathered from flowers is an important carbohydrate source for bees; however, if they stored it in this form, bacteria and molds would soon spoil the nectar. Thus, bees add an enzyme (invertase) that converts nectar to honey, in which mold and bacteria cannot grow. In addition, bees fan the converted nectar to dry it out and make it too thick for yeast to grow. They also add some more enzymes that convert a small portion of the honey to hydrogen peroxide, which acts as an effective antibiotic. All of the above tactics prevent the honey from spoiling and insures a food supply for the queen and the colony.

In addition to nectar, bees gather pollen by packing it into "baskets" located on the hind legs. Pollen is an important source of protein, without which bees would not be able to produce offspring. Have you ever seen bees with clumps of yellow pollen attached to their back legs? It looks like they have two saddle bags.

By producing nectar and pollen, plants are not just being altruistic to bees. Plants benefit from foraging bees because they transfer pollen to other flowering plants. This promotes fertilization, which would otherwise be more difficult by merely spreading pollen in the wind. Bees pollinate a variety of plants, and flowers are specifically designed to attract these insects. Regardless of the enjoyment we (humans) get from flowers, these colorful objects were designed primarily to attract insects for plant reproduction.

Natural Life History of Honey Bees

A beehive is first started by a swarm of bees (including one queen) that have left an overcrowded or destroyed beehive. Swarming usually occurs in the spring or summer when flowers are plentiful. After locating a suitable site, the workers produce wax and build sheets of combs that are an intricate part of a bee hive. Wax combs contain cells that hold pollen, honey, and young bee larvae. Workers, which are sterile females, do a variety of activities depending on the age of the individual. Young bees clean cells, produce wax, and nurse the young and the queen. As they grow older, workers shift to guarding and foraging duties.

Eggs laid by the queen hatch in three days and develop into adults in about seventeen days. Fertilized eggs mature into female workers, and unfertilized eggs into male drones; periodically, queen bees are produced when certain larvae are fed "royal jelly" over the course of their development. Emerging queens will battle each other to the death with only one remaining queen to lay eggs for the colony. (The original queen has already left the hive to start another colony or has died). Why do new queens battle each other to the death?

Bees gather nectar and pollen throughout the flowering season, and when winter comes, the colony goes into a dormant state and lives off the stored honey. Bees warm the hive by "shivering" their wing muscles much like we do when we are cold!

Fun Things to Do with Honey Bees

I would suggest consulting with an expert beekeeper if you are inclined to raise bees. Many people are allergic to bee stings, and should not mess with them. Beekeeping can be a fun, enterprising adventure, but it is difficult, time consuming, and potentially dangerous. You really have to be dedicated to take on this project.

You can observe bees in their natural habitat without constructing a beehive. Hundreds of different species of bees exist in North America. Their foraging activities are fascinating and fun to watch. You can safely watch them up close as long as you do not disturb them too much. When observing bees, take careful notes. How long does a bee, on average, spend at each particular flower? Do they seem to prefer certain species of flowers? Why?

Can bees see color? Train bees on a certain color by providing sugared water at a colored feeding station; then offer them several feeding stations with a variety of colors (all the same food) and see whether they chose the color you trained them on.

Put out an artificial flower with a sugar solution in it. How long does it take for a bee to discover it? How long before other bees go to it? Change the shape, color, and location of the flower. What type of flower do the bees prefer? Make some hypotheses (calculated predictions), and I'll bet you will come up with many new experiments.

Common Honey Bees
Hit by Cars and Trucks

☐ **COMMON HONEY BEE (*Apis mellifera*)**

Local distribution:

These insects are encountered on most roads in the spring, summer, and fall.

Eggs and larvae:

Eggs and larvae are found in hives usually located in tree hollows and other dry crevices.

Adults:

Adults are gold and black and are distinguished from hover flies because bees have four wings.

HORSE AND DEER FLIES

ORDER: DIPTERA
FAMILY: TABANIDAE

F lies in this family are fierce biters and due to their size (up to 25 mm), they can inflict pain. As with most biting insects, only females bite and both sexes feed on flower nectar. There are about 300 species in North America.

Adults commonly hang out around water. I am sure that people who swim in rivers, springs, and lakes are quite familiar with these biting flies. I can recall many a time when my peaceful, relaxing trip on an inner tube down a river had been interrupted by an obnoxious horse fly trying to bite me. Even worse, smaller deer flies are silent, and you do not notice their presence until they have already taken a big chunk out of you!

One story claims that because horse flies in Philadelphia were biting so fiercely in the summer of 1776, the delegates decided to sign the Declaration of Independence by July 4 just to get away from them! Just think, if horse flies were not around, we might be celebrating Independence Day in August!

Natural Life History of Horse and Deer Flies

Surprisingly, not much is known about the biology of flies in this family. You can tell a male from a female by the eyes—female eyes have a space between them whereas male eyes do not (see Plate XV).

A majority of the species in this family lay large batches of eggs in or near water. Larvae are thought to be carnivorous, eating almost any small organism and also each other. Although living in water, these larvae do not have gill-like structures to extract oxygen from the water, and need to come to the surface to acquire oxygen.

Fun Things to Do with Horse and Deer Flies

You can learn new things about the life cycle of these flies if you can find their eggs, which is the difficult part. Try searching boggy places around the base of trees. Also, you can use yourself as bait and trap a female, hopefully full of eggs and ready to lay.

When you go hunting for fly eggs, you will probably find many other types of eggs. When you place them in an aquarium, group similar eggs together and separate each group with a Plexiglas® divider. Be sure to keep a fine mesh lid on the aquarium. Take careful notes about what the eggs look like, where you found them, how long it takes for the eggs to hatch, and what the larvae look like. You may even discover a new species!

I'd name my pet horse fly "Jaws!"

Common Horse and Deer Flies Hit by Cars and Trucks

☐ **COMMON HORSE (Genus: *Tabanus*) and**

☐ **DEER FLIES (Genus: *Chrysops*)**

Local distribution:

These insects are encountered on most roads during the day throughout the summer.

Eggs and larvae:

Eggs and larvae are found mostly in water.

Adults:

Adults are quite common outdoors, around bodies of water.

· HOVER FLIES ·

ORDER: DIPTERA
FAMILY: SYRPHIDAE

Can you imagine keeping your body motionless in midair? Well, the flies of the family Syrphidae have perfected the art of hovering flight. You have seen these flies hovering around flowers, wings beating so fast that you cannot see them. If you approach one, they will dart away in almost any direction.

Most people mistakenly identify a hover fly as a honey bee or a wasp. After all, most hover flies have yellow and black stripes on the abdomen. But these flies cannot sting. The way to distinguish hover flies from bees or wasps is to count their wings. Hover flies have only two, whereas bees and wasps have four. (But be careful, many wasps have two wings that are very small and difficult to see.) Why do you think these flies mimic bees and wasps?

Comparatively little is known about the biology and ecology of hover flies. This provides a unique opportunity for almost anybody to go out and study these critters.

Natural Life History of Hover Flies

Males are generally smaller than females, and both sexes have large eyes. They are acrobatic fliers with their wings reportedly moving up and down 250 times per second!

Hover flies feed primarily on nectar and pollen from flowers, but they also lap up honeydew from the surface of leaves. Honeydew, by the way, is produced by plant-feeding aphids (small insects in the order Homoptera). Hover flies do not possess an elongated proboscis like butterflies; however, some hover flies do have pointed faces that allow them to get to the pollen and nectar of a flower.

Males of most species actively search for females, usually in areas where females feed or lay eggs. But some males are known to hover in swarms and wait for females to visit. Females of some species (e.g., the drone fly) have the ability to overwinter in the adult stage. Thus, emerging hover flies in the spring may be old females; you can recognize old females by their tattered appearance.

Once mated, females store sperm in their abdomen and seek out places to lay the eggs. Some hover flies (e.g., the drone fly) lay eggs in stagnant, smelly water; others (e.g., genus *Syrphus*) lay their eggs on plants containing aphid populations; and some (e.g., genus *Volucella*) lay their eggs in the nests of bumblebees and wasps. Hover fly eggs are normally oval, and they hatch within five days.

Larvae (i.e., maggots) are usually white or a brown-yellow, long and thin, and they molt four times before emerging as an adult. Larvae of various species eat all kinds of things: plant juices, decaying matter in water, stuff discarded by bees and wasps in their nests, or aphids. Farmers have been extremely interested in hover fly larvae that eat aphids, mainly because many species of aphids eat fruit and vegetable crops.

Fun Things to Do with Hover Flies

As mentioned earlier, the biology and ecology of hover flies is unknown for many species, so many new things can be done with these insects. Plus, they are just attractive insects to catch and observe!

You can catch hover flies with butterfly nets if you are exceptionally quick. Stalk them in any garden or field that contains an assortment of white and yellow flowers. If you catch a female (sometimes you can see the eggs in her abdomen), place her in a cage with appropriate food for the larvae; she will soon deposit the eggs. Alternatively, you can search for larvae in their natural habitat, such as plants with lots of aphids.

Depending on what species of hover fly you have, you will have to raise them in different ways. Provide aphid-eating larvae with plenty of aphids, and place some sand or soil in the cage for the larvae to pupate in. For aquatic species, keep them in a dish containing the water in which you found them, and sink the dish into some soil; you can feed them decaying animal parts. You can even obtain dead animals along the side of a road, but be careful, you might have to fight off some vultures!

To get hover flies to mate, you need to build a rather large cage (i.e., 1 m × 1 m × 1 m) stocked with plenty of flowers. When observing the larvae, take careful notes.

You can also observe hover flies in their natural surroundings. Here are some questions you can answer through observation. Do males search for females or do they hang out in groups? Do the males defend territories? What type of flowers do hover flies prefer? What time during the day do they normally feed? If you find aphid-eating larvae...what species of aphid do the larvae eat? How do they attack the aphids? How quickly do the larvae move? Can some aphids escape? You can come up with many more questions. You can also build up an impressive hover fly collection (see section on how to preserve insects). They are truly beautiful insects!

I like the little orange ones.

Common Hover Flies Hit by Cars and Trucks

☐ DRONE FLIES (Genus: *Eristalis*)

Local distribution:

One can encounter drone flies on all roads during the daytime in the spring and summer.

Eggs and larvae:

Eggs and larvae are found in rotting matter and "foul water." Larvae have a long tail which is used to acquire air (larvae are called rat-tailed maggots).

Adults:

Adults resemble honey bees and are found in gardens and meadows.

Interesting facts:

Drone flies are thought to prefer yellow flowers (e.g., chrysanthemums or asters) and are important pollinators for many plants because of their hairy bodies. When you catch one in a net, they will produce a loud buzzing sound. Don't be fooled! It is pretending to be an angry bee.

Females can survive through a winter, and they will lay fertilized eggs upon emerging in the spring. Interestingly, one species of larvae, *E. tenax*, reportedly gives "birth" to another larvae before entering the adult stage!

☐ SYRPHUS FLIES (Genus: *Syrphus*)

Local distribution:

You can encounter these flies on most roads, excluding Texas, Oklahoma, Arizona, Nevada, New Mexico, and Utah) during the daytime in the spring and summer.

Eggs and larvae:

Eggs and larvae are found on plants with large aphid populations.

Adults:

Adults resemble hairy bees.

Interesting facts:

Have you ever been walking through the woods and heard a high-pitched whine in the bushes next to you? This noise is produced by a male syrphus fly who is attempting to warm himself up. If you listen closely, the pitch will rise with his temperature. You can approach fairly close to a male, and they will sometimes even land on the end on your finger.

The larvae of this species are voracious predators of aphids. Most are active at night. They whip their heads down on unsuspecting aphids, grasp them with their mouthparts, and proceed to suck the juice out. Although they are ferocious predators of aphids, the larvae can become prey to parasitic wasps. The wasps lay eggs within the body of the fly larvae and upon hatching, wasp larvae eat out the insides of their hosts (what a way to go!). As a defense mechanism, larvae react to a wasp's touch by rolling off the leaf, sometimes escaping the wasp's advances.

☐ VOLUCELLA FLIES (Genus: *Volucella*)

Local distribution:

One can encounter these flies on roads in the northeast and southeast regions of the U.S. (including Texas and Kansas) during the daytime in spring, summer, and sometimes fall.

Eggs and larvae:

Eggs and larvae are found in nests of bees and wasps.

Adults:

Adults resemble bees and wasps.

Interesting facts:

Hover flies in this genus are extremely fast and difficult to see clearly. Being good mimics of bumblebees and wasps, many people mistake this hover fly for the real thing. However, hover flies in this genus do not fool bees or wasps. In fact, wasps have been known to attack Volucella if they appear on the wasps' nest. To avoid an attack, a female Volucella uses a guerrilla tactic. At dusk, she sneaks in and lays her eggs on the edge of the nest.

Once the eggs hatch, larvae go to the bottom of the nest to feed on debris discarded by the wasps (i.e., dead wasp grubs), and they may even feed on the excrement of wasp grubs. Apparently, once in the nest, *Volucella* larvae are not attacked by the adult wasps. Hmmm…I wonder why? Maybe the larvae produce a chemical that tells the wasp not to attack it or they take on the smell of the nest.

· JUMPING PLANT LICE ·

ORDER: HOMOPTERA
FAMILY: PSYLLIDAE
GENUS: PACHYPSYLLA

The larvae of jumping plant lice feed on the sap of plants and produce recognizable galls on the leaves and stems. If you have ever looked at the leaves of a sugarberry tree (*Celtis laevigata*) or hackberry trees, which are quite common in the eastern and central part of the U.S., you may have noticed a number of funny-shaped growths on the leaves. These galls come in various shapes: nipple, dome, virus-like, and fuzzy. Take a look at a sugarberry tree, you will know what I mean. Most jumping plant lice are host-specific. In other words, each species only feeds on a particular plant. The jumping plant lice that produce galls on hackberry trees are in the genus *Pachypsylla*.

Natural Life History of Jumping Plant Lice

Relative to the larvae, not much is known about the adults. Both sexes hunker-down in the bark of sugarberry or hackberry trees during the winter. In the spring, females oviposit on the leaves and buds. Adults are called jumping plant lice because they possess strong hindlegs that enable them to leap from leaf to leaf.

The eggs hatch into microscopic nymphs, called "crawlers." Crawlers wander over vegetation, in search of a suitable site in which to settle. Once they have picked a spot, they insert their mouth parts (called a "stylet") and feed on the juice in the leaves.

Developing leaves react to the presence of the nymphs in a most unusual way. The tissues of the developing leaf actually grow over the nymphs, forming a hollow ball (called a gall). Although it is not clearly known how leaves form galls, it is thought that the saliva of jumping plant lice stimulate leaf tissues to grow a particular way. By the way, what do you think the purpose of a gall is to the insect?

The nymphs molt within the gall an unknown number of times to reach the adult stage. Adults saw their way out of the gall and fly out, leaving the gall intact. Adults are very small (2 to 5 mm). They resemble miniature cicadas, but they can jump from leaf to leaf.

Fun Things to Do with Jumping Plant Lice

Little is known about these secretive, but familiar insects. The larvae produce many different kinds of galls on sugarberry trees. I would like to know whether different species construct different types of galls or the larvae of the same species produce all types of galls? This would be quite interesting because nobody really knows. You can locate the galls on sugarberry or hackberry trees. These trees are easily identified by the bunch of little knobs that occur on the bark.

To determine which species hatch from each type of gall, separate the different types of galls found on the leaves of different branches by placing fine netting around them. Do not break off the branches of the tree, because the leaves will dry up and the larvae will die. Now take careful notes. How long does it take for the adults to emerge? Do they all emerge at once? Are the insects that emerge from each particular gall a different species (i.e., do they look different)? How do they respond to various stimuli, such as light, temperature, and wind? What the heck do the adults eat, or do they eat at all? Are the sexes colored or shaped differently? You can tell a female primarily when she is full of eggs. Do they lay their eggs in the summer or do they wait until the next spring? You can discover many new and exciting behaviors of these insects through careful observation.

If you have a sugarberry or hackberry tree nearby, you can make other novel observations about jumping plant lice. When do the virus, nipple, dome, and fuzzy galls appear on the leaves? Do they occur at the same time? Careful, remember the adults can hatch out and leave the galls intact, look for a small hole to see if a particular gall is empty. Open up a few of the different kinds of galls, and observe the larvae under a microscope. What do they look like? Why do you think the larvae make the leaves form galls? Remove a nymph from its gall and observe it. What does it do after it is removed from its home?

Jumping Plant Lice Hit by Cars and Trucks

☐ **JUMPING PLANT LICE (Genus: *Pachypsylla*)**

Local distribution:

These insects are encountered on most central and eastern roads in the spring, summer, and fall.

Eggs and larvae:

Larvae construct galls specifically on the leaves of sugarberry and hackberry trees.

Adults:

Adults are small with delicate wings.

· LACEWINGS ·
ORDER: NEUROPTERA
FAMILY: CHRYSOPIDAE

Lacewings are common insects in North America, where there are eighty-seven species. They are usually greenish in color and can be found in grasses, shrubs, and trees. Lacewing larvae feed on aphids and even insect pests, such as the citrus whitefly.

Although adult lacewings appear to be delicate creatures, the larvae are ferocious predators of aphids (which are plant lice in the order Aphididae). However, several species of ants love aphid honeydew, and protect aphids from all potential predators, including lacewing larvae. Some lacewing larvae go so far as to attach organic debris, such as pieces of lichen, on their backs. This may be an attempt by lacewing larvae to disguise themselves from the guarding ants, permitting the larvae to sneak in and attack aphids!

Natural Life History of Lacewings

Adults are nocturnal and are found underneath leaves during the day. At night, they feed on honeydew and possibly other small insects. Females lay eggs on the leaves of shrubs. The eggs are laid on the end of long, spindly stalks, constructed by the female. (Why do they oviposit on the ends of a stalk?) Larvae are mobile, and will attack any soft-bodied insect they encounter. Most species molt approximately two times, after which the larvae spin a cocoon on leaves or between rough bark ridges. Interestingly, the lacewing emerges from the cocoon in a pupal form, then molts into an adult. Larvae develop into adults in about twenty-five days.

Fun Things to Do with Lacewings

There are many unknowns about these insects. Collect the larvae or eggs on bushes in the spring or fall (find bushes infested with aphids). Once collected, place the larvae in separate jars, because they are cannibalistic and will eat each other. Adults can be collected around bright lights at night. Direct observations of larval development and behavior would be quite interesting. For example, how long does it take for lacewing larvae to emerge as adults?

Also, a fun experiment would be to determine if debris-covered lacewing larvae can really fool ants. You can do the experiment in a cage, or more easily, you can conduct the experiment on a bush. You will have many trials and errors before you come up with an appropriate experimental design. I would try to find larvae that are covered with debris. When you find some, see if there are ants nearby guarding aphids. Can these debris-covered larvae successfully capture aphids despite ants being close by?

Hey!...Would you look at that Lacewing...

Shhh...It's a ferocious predator in search of honeydew!

Common Lacewings Hit by Cars and Trucks

☐ **COMMON LACEWINGS (Genus: *Chrysopa*)**

Local distribution:

These insects are encountered on most roads at night, especially in the spring and summer.

Eggs and larvae:

C. rufilabris & *C. oculata* eggs are laid on fabricated, long, spindly stalks attached to the undersides of leaves. Larvae construct cocoons.

Adults:

Adults are green with long, delicate wings (approximately 13 mm in length).

· LOVEBUGS ·

ORDER: DIPTERA
FAMILY: BIBIONIDAE
GENUS: PLECIA
SPECIES: NEARCTICA AND AMERICANA

Motorists in the Gulf Coast states cannot help but notice this insect. Lovebugs congregate around roads, especially in May and September, and practically cover the front ends of cars, clogging up radiators and covering windshields. Lovebug residue left on cars for an extended period of time eats away at the paint, leaving marks shaped similar to the splat left on the car. Lovebugs are not true bugs (true bugs are in the order Hemiptera), but whenever people see these insects, the male and female are attached to each other flying around in tandem; hence the name "lovebug." What a life—most of your adulthood spent attached to a member of the opposite sex!

There are two species of lovebugs in the Southeast, *P. nearctica* and *P. americana*. The former is the species people encounter on highways, whereas the latter is normally a woodland species and does not fly around highways in such huge numbers. It is difficult to tell the difference between the two. Both species are black with reddish-orange thoraxes, but *P. nearctica*'s thorax is not completely red-orange whereas the thorax of *P. americana* is completely red-orange. *P. nearctica* emerges in large numbers in May and September, and can be seen only in the months of April, May, and June; thus, lovebugs seen in the fall are all *P. nearctica*.

Another insect, *Dilophus sayi* (family Bibionidae) is a species that many people confuse with a lovebug. *D. sayi* adults fly around in tandem and are also attracted to parked cars and even barbecue grills. These insects are smaller than lovebugs, and they have an all black body that lacks the reddish-orange colored thorax. Although numerous from

January to April, *D. sayi* are not a major nuisance to motorists on most highways.

But where did *P. nearctica* (alias, "the lovebug") come from? *P. nearctica* was first recorded in Louisiana as early as 1911 (possibly migrating from Central America) and has since spread to most of the Gulf Coast states. The lovebug is thought to have invaded Florida in the late 1940s and then spread to the Carolinas. Because it is so common, hereafter, I will only be talking about the lovebug species *P. nearctica*.

These are my favorite bugs!

What attracts lovebugs to highways? Researchers have reported that ultraviolet light (UV) combined with automobile exhaust fumes seems to attract lovebugs. Interestingly, UV light or exhaust fumes alone do not appeal to lovebugs. Exhaust fumes must be irradiated with UV light for it to work. On the highways, lovebugs can usually be found between 10 AM and 4 PM, when incidence of UV light is high. Formaldehyde and heptaldehyde are the two most attractive components in irradiated exhaust fumes. (I wonder if there is a way to remove these two components from gasoline so as not to attract lovebugs.) Hot engines and automobile vibrations may also contribute to attracting lovebugs.

I know what you are thinking . . . Why the heck are lovebugs attracted to automobile exhaust fumes? Well, let's look at the natural behavior of lovebugs. In nature, female lovebugs prefer to lay their eggs in decaying organic matter. Females locate decaying organic matter by the odor it releases. This odor happens to contain the same components that are found in irradiated exhaust fumes (i.e., heptaldehyde). For thousands of years, lovebugs have been attracted to decaying organic matter in order to deposit eggs, but now millions of automobiles are producing odors that mimic the smell of decaying organic matter, and lovebugs are lured to a most unpleasant egg-laying site. What an unfortunate situation for both humans and lovebugs! It would be interesting to see if lovebugs ever learn to avoid highways or if humans develop and use alternative fuel sources.

What is it about lovebugs that causes the paint on cars to be eaten away? It is partly because the body fluids of lovebugs are slightly acidic. However, most of the damage results when the lovebugs are left on the car for a few days; bacterial activity increases the acidity and this eats the paint. Wash your car immediately after a lovebug confrontation!

Because there are so many lovebugs, one would think these insects would provide a feast for most birds; however, birds apparently find these insects distasteful. The reddish-orange thorax warns birds that lovebugs are not good to eat. A naive bird might try one lovebug once, but only once! I guess the automobiles may be the only "predator" of lovebugs.

You might be thinking, "What the heck is good about a lovebug?" They are not eaten by anything and are just a nuisance on highways. Well, Mother Nature does not care about the usefulness of insects by human standards. If an insect can survive and reproduce, it will be present in the environment. Further, lovebugs may play an important ecological role. For example, lovebug larvae eat organic matter and may actually recycle organic waste. Additionally, other animals may actually prey on lovebug larvae. You cannot think of different species as separate entities, because each species plays an intricate role in an ecological community (even though most of the time humans do not understand this role).

Natural Life History of Lovebugs

Males and females live three to six days. The males tend to outlive the females. Most of their time is spent mating. Males search for females by hovering 0.3 to 0.9 meters above the ground in grassy areas, usually in the morning and early evening. Females hang out in the vegetation, waiting for the right moment to fly into a swarm of males. Once detected, a female is immediately grasped by a male. Sometimes several males and one female fall to the vegetation below. A battle ensues among the many encircling males and in these contests, larger males usually win. Copulating pairs fly about, attached for an average of fifty-six hours (Wow! Why so long?) and are known to fly as high as 1,500 feet! Coupled lovebugs are so numerous that at times they have been estimated to cover one-quarter the land area in the State of Florida! Once separated, a female lays eggs in suitable rotting vegetation (such as decaying leaves) and subsequently dies.

The larvae of lovebugs are gray with hairlike projections on their bodies and have dark heads. A full-grown larva is approximately 11 to 12 mm long.

Fun Things to Do with Lovebugs

Almost nothing has been reported about the larval stage of the lovebug, so basic observations would be interesting. Collect a few pairs of lovebugs (which are easy to catch during the months of May and September), and place them in a suitable cage. Provide the female with suitable larvae habitat, such as moist, decaying sod with lots of leaves.

Now sit back and observe. How long does it take the eggs to hatch? How many hatched? How long does it take for the larvae to mature? How many times do the larvae molt? What are their reactions to light—do they avoid it or move towards it? What about temperature—what is their reaction to hot or cold? Why do you think it is important that the larvae react to different stimuli? You can also vary the type of vegetation and soil in the cage and find out what the larvae prefer.

A question that has popped into my mind is whether *P. americana* and *D. sayi* are just as distasteful to birds as *P. nearctica*. You can design several experiments to test this question. Try feeding them to a pet bird. (Use only those birds that are known to eat insects.) I don't think this experiment has been done. It would be interesting to see which species is the most distasteful to birds.

You can also observe courting males in the field. In the late evening (in May or September), sit down in the middle of a field and pretty soon you will see tons of males hovering above the vegetation around you. These males are battling for position to mate with a female in the vegetation below.

Common Lovebugs Hit by Cars and Trucks

☐ COMMON LOVEBUG (*Plecia nearctica*)

Local distribution:

This lovebug is encountered on most roads in the Southeast during the day, primarily in May and September.

Eggs and larvae:

Eggs are deposited by the female in decaying vegetation. Full-grown larvae are 11 to 12 mm long and gray with a dark head.

Adults:

Males and females are usually seen flying in tandem (13 to 15 mm long) along highways.

· MIDGES ·

ORDER: DIPTERA
FAMILY: CHIRONOMIDAE

Although the species in this family do not bite, they are quite familiar to people because they form huge swarms in the early evening. Midges resemble small mosquitoes, but lack the biting mouthparts. There are over 670 species of midges in North America. The females of a few species are known to reproduce parthenogenetically, meaning they can lay unfertilized eggs that hatch successfully. In fact, in some species, no male offspring exists, just females!

Natural Life History of Midges

Adults are normally smaller than 10 mm and live for only a few days, just enough time to reproduce. Like biting midges, male midges swarm for mating purposes, waiting for females to fly through.

Females oviposit in water or moist vegetation. Eggs of aquatic species are strung together in strings, and are seen floating on top of the water in small gelatinous masses. Larvae are scavengers and many live underwater in tubes or cases composed of organic matter. Midge larvae are numerous and are important prey for fish and other aquatic animals.

Fun Things to Do with Midges

Because not much is known about the life cycle of many midge species, you can gather eggs from ponds and discover new information by observing them in an aquarium. For instance, how long does it take for the eggs to hatch? What is the length of a larval stage? the pupae stage? How do they react to light? You will learn many new things from simple observations. Take careful notes! Much of the stuff you learn, nobody else knows. Share some of your observations with entomologists in your community.

Common Midges Hit by Cars and Trucks

☐ **COMMON MIDGES (Family: Chironomidae)**

Local distribution:

These insects are encountered on most roads during the early evening in the spring, summer, and fall.

Eggs and larvae:

Eggs and larvae are found in various small ponds. Larvae are completely aquatic.

Adults:

Adults are medium-sized, gray, and resemble small mosquitoes.

·MOLE CRICKETS·

ORDER: ORTHOPTERA
FAMILY: GRYLLOTALPIDAE

What the heck is a mole cricket? I remember when I first came to the South, I asked the same question. However, most cattlemen, turf managers, golf course managers, and home owners with big lawns know what a mole cricket is. They are pests found in grasses and many gardens. Their habit of tunneling and feeding on the roots of many plants causes significant damage. In fact, the annual cost of mole cricket damage has been estimated to be 30 million dollars annually, just in Florida.

The first time I encountered a mole cricket, I was playing tennis at night around the end of April. I was retrieving a ball when I observed this rather strange insect walking right in front of me. It looked like some prehistoric monster! It was 55 mm (2 inches) long and had large, serrated forelegs which were obviously digging tools. During the course of the tennis match, many more of these insects appeared on the court, and they actually became quite a nuisance.

Seven species of mole crickets occur in North America, but only three are of economic significance: the tawny (*Scapteriscus vicinus*), the southern (*Scapteriscus acletus*), and the short-winged (*Scapteriscus abbreviatus*) mole cricket. All three of these pests were introduced to the Southeast in the 1900s, most likely traveling on ships from South America. The northern mole cricket, *Neocurilla hexadactyla*, is native and is reported not to cause as much damage to turf as the other three species. To differentiate between the northern and the three introduced mole crickets, observe the end of the abdomen: the northern has much longer cerci (two tail-like projections on the end of the abdomen) than the other three species.

Natural Life History of Mole Crickets

Mole crickets will feed on almost any plant, including vegetables, sugar-cane, ornamentals, and tobacco seedlings; they will also eat small insects. Mole crickets spend most of their life underground, feeding on the roots of plants; however, at night, mole crickets are known to leave their bur-rows and bite off the stems and leaves of plants.

Sometimes mole crickets, especially the tawny and southern, will fly about in large numbers. They have been known to fly up to two miles. The purpose of these flights is to find new food resources and mates. Like other crickets, male crickets sing to attract females. Males sing shortly after sunset for about one hour. Males produce the song by rubbing their uniquely shaped hind legs together. Each male's song only attracts females of the same species. But unlike other crickets that sing above ground, male mole crickets construct a most unusual burrow designed specifically to amplify their calls. Have you ever cupped your hands around your mouth to amplify your voice? Male mole crickets, not having the luxury of hands, build a horn-like chamber underground with two openings at the soil surface. During construction, males will peri-odically sing and then change part of the burrow. Apparently males are "tuning" their burrows to get just the right sound! I guess the better (or louder) a male's song sounds, the more females he will attract.

A female flying in the vicinity of a calling male will respond and enter the male's chamber. Once a female has entered, she will fight with the male to make him stop calling. (Why do you think she does this?) The male then begins a series of courtship maneuvers. When the female is receptive, the male produces a spermato-phore (a package of sperm) in about forty seconds. Females will either eat the spermatophore or use it to fertilize her eggs. Females have been known to copulate with the same male several times, but when a female does not respond to the male's courtship, the male forces her out of the burrow and begins singing again.

After obtaining a spermatophore, a female will fly off in search of a suitable egg-laying site. Digging a small egg chamber (4 × 3 cm) in the soil, she proceeds to lay about forty eggs. Once finished, the female will seal the opening and fly away to lay another clutch of eggs or mate with another male. Mole cricket eggs usually hatch within twenty days, and the young tunnel up to the surface. Nymphs resemble tiny adults but without wings.

Currently, research is being done on how to control mole cricket populations. Both biological (e.g., digger wasps that eat mole crickets) and chemical (e.g., malathion bait) control methods are being used to reduce mole cricket populations. Contact your local pest control operator for more information.

Fun Things to Do with Mole Crickets

The unique calling behavior of these insects makes them particularly interesting to study. You can capture mole crickets in the spring and fall around lighted areas (e.g., tennis courts, in which case most of them will be tawny and southern mole crickets). Go ahead and pick them up with your hands, they will not bite. Now, place them in buckets with plenty of moist soil and vegetation; be sure to cover the top with some sort of screen so they will not escape. Try to separate the males from the females (only males sing and they have a harp-like structure near the base of the wing). Once separated, you can observe how the males construct their singing chambers. Observe the mole crickets under low levels of light or they will not behave normally. You can also try a yellow or red light (many insects cannot see yellow or red) and maybe they will not react so much to it.

Now, listen. Do males make different chirping noises? Do some males sing louder than other males? Tawny males make "buzzy" noises and have silent periods lasting less than one second, whereas southern mole cricket sounds are more musical and continuous. Put some females in with calling males. What do the females do? Now place a male in with another male; does the singing male change its song? What do you think the singing male is trying to communicate? You can even place a calling male in your backyard and see how many females fly down to the bucket.

Fill a mole cricket's singing chamber with plaster to determine what it looks like. (You will be amazed!) Compare chambers of different species. Change the shape of a chamber, and see how it affects the song. Place different species of mole crickets in chambers constructed by other species. Do they sing or do they spend most of their time trying to fix the burrow? Do different species construct different chambers (a most interesting question!)?

If you have a gravid (pregnant) female, place her in a separate bucket and wait for her to lay eggs (sometimes it will take nine to fourteen days). Place the egg chamber in a see-through container. How long does it take the eggs to hatch? How many times do the larvae molt before becoming adults with wings? How do they respond to light? to heat? to temperature? to moisture? Why do larvae respond the way they do? Because the developing stage in a mole cricket's life is poorly understood, many researchers might be interested in your observations.

Common Mole Crickets Hit by Cars and Trucks

☐ **TAWNY MOLE CRICKET (*Scapteriscus vicinus*)**

☐ **SOUTHERN MOLE CRICKET (*Scapteriscus acletus*)**

☐ **SHORT-WINGED MOLE CRICKET (*Scapteriscus abbreviatus*) and**

☐ **NORTHERN MOLE CRICKET (*Neocurilla hexadactyla*)**

Local distribution:

The northern mole cricket is encountered on roads in both the Southeast and Northeast, whereas the other species are located only in the Southeast. Mole crickets fly at night, especially in the spring and fall.

Eggs and larvae:

Eggs are deposited in moist soil, 9 to 30 cm deep. Juveniles molt six or seven times.

Adults:

Females are usually seen flying at night during the spring and fall, especially after a rainstorm.

· MOSQUITOES ·
ORDER: DIPTERA
FAMILY: CULICIDAE

Mosquito is a Spanish word that means "little fly," but what a fly! Everybody knows the mosquito. These insects seem to have an insatiable lust for blood, and they inflict painful bites that leave itchy red bumps. People visiting the Florida Everglades swear these insects are so numerous, they could practically carry you away.

What is the purpose of these pesky insects? Frequently I have heard people (myself included) say, "Mosquitoes are just a nuisance. . . I wish we could get rid of every single one!" However, for several species of animals, mosquitoes are an important food item. Several species of bird, bat, insect, snail, and fish feed on adult mosquitoes and their larvae. For example, the brown bat (*Myotis lucifugus*) feeds on mosquitoes at night. If you want to get rid of some mosquitoes, build a few bat houses on your property! A couple of bats flying around your yard will help control the population of mosquitoes. Do not worry about bats flying into your hair (a popular myth); they are equipped with excellent ultrasonic equipment and can readily avoid you.

Natural Life History of Mosquitoes

Did you know that only female mosquitoes thirst for blood? Males normally feed on plant nectar and fruits, but females require animal blood for the development of their eggs. You can tell the differences between a male and female without waiting to see which one bites you. If you have some well-preserved specimens on your windshield or grill, look at the antennae. Males have larger, hairier antennae than females. Furthermore, males have two large claspers that look like two hooks on the tip of the abdomen. You can observe them with the aid of a micro-scope. These claspers are used to grasp the female during mating.

But how does a male mosquito recognize a female? In humans, certain anatomical characteristics allow us to distinguish between the sexes. But a male mosquito does not find females by sight. He locates a female primarily by the sound of her wings. In flight, females produce sounds that range between 300 and 800 vibrations per second. The sound of a flying female is music to any male mosquito. In fact, males will be lured in by any source that produces this range of sounds (including a tuning fork).

Mating usually occurs shortly after mosquitoes emerge as adults from their larval sites. A male has to be fairly close to a female in order to detect her (within a foot) with his antennae. Once he finds her, the male quickly grasps the female's abdomen with his legs, and the couple perform an intricate copulatory act lasting about seventeen seconds. After copulation, the female mosquito does something extraordinarily interesting with the sperm. She stores it in her abdomen for the duration of her life and controls the fertilization of her own eggs. Thus once mated, a female can lay fertilized eggs for the rest of her life!

Carrying fertilized eggs, a female will actively search for a "blood meal." (Yes, entomologists use this term.) The protein in blood is essential in the production of yolk, which provides nutrients for young mosquitoes. Some species of mosquitoes can lay their first batch of eggs without blood, but they still need blood for subsequent broods. To obtain blood, females possess long, pointed mouthparts that penetrate the skin of an animal. Females are able to suck up the blood by injecting saliva into the wound, which dilutes the blood and makes it easier to withdraw. This saliva also causes nearby blood capillaries to dilate, enhancing blood flow. But what makes you itch? If you haven't guessed already...mosquito saliva is the stuff that causes itchy, red bumps on the skin.

A female that has obtained some blood (without first being squashed!) is ready to lay her eggs and will search for an appropriate site. All mosquito eggs require some amount of water in order for the eggs to hatch, so females explore any water-containing receptacle. Females briefly land on top of the water to determine the suitability of the site. Female mosquitoes have small hairs on their legs that can tell how salty the water is. (Most species prefer fresh water, but a few prefer brackish water.) However, some species deposit their eggs in areas subject to flooding during heavy rains. These eggs will develop when the water level is high.

After locating a favorable site, a female lays whitish eggs at the edge of a water reservoir. Deposited into the water, the eggs swell and turn dark. They usually hatch into larvae within two days. A larva pops the top off the egg by pushing the wall of it with a small spine located on top of its head. (It's kind of like opening the hatch of a circular submarine.) Breaking the egg wall, a larva squirms out, takes a deep breath, and immediately searches for food.

But how do larvae breathe and what do they eat? Larvae cannot extract oxygen from the water, so they have specially designed breathing apparatuses. Some species have tube-like structures that poke through the surface of the water, whereas other species have structures that extract oxygen trapped in plant cells underneath the water. Isn't that amazing? Mosquito larvae that acquire oxygen from plant cells! Larvae feed on a wide variety of things, including algae, protozoa, bacteria, and yeasts.

Development from egg to adult takes approximately six to fifteen days, depending on the species. Larvae are small and wiggle end over end in the water when disturbed. Most larvae molt four times. After the fourth molt, larvae become an active, comma-shaped pupae. The pupae do not feed, and they usually just float near the surface; however, they will dive down to the bottom with mad jerking motions when disturbed. Most mosquito larvae and pupae react to shadows passing over themselves or when the container in which they are in is observed. If you find a container full of mosquito larvae, make ripples in the water and watch all of the mosquitoes scramble downward!

Have you ever wondered how mosquitoes survive the winter? Well, most adult mosquitoes do not survive (except for a few species), but their eggs do. Mosquito eggs are tolerant to freezes and after many months of cold temperatures, they will hatch when spring arrives. In fact, some mosquitoes lay eggs in the middle of summer that do not hatch until the next spring, even though environmental conditions are favorable during the summer. This sudden cessation of development is known as "diapause." Diapause is regulated by internal factors (i.e. hormones) instead of external factors (i.e., climate).

Regarding the control of mosquitoes, a majority of those that bite you around your house can be eliminated by removing receptacles that hold water for an extended length of time. For example, one domestic mosquito (*Aedes aegypti*) primarily lays eggs in temporary containers such as tires, cans, and flower vases. This species flies no more than 100 yards from its birth site. You can rid yourself of their presence by simply removing all potential water containers on your property.

Some people use much more extravagant measures to get rid of mosquitoes. Many home owners use ultraviolet light or blacklight electrocution traps. However, these devices *will not significantly reduce the number of biting mosquitoes in your yard*. Don't buy them; they are a waste of money! Most importantly, these traps kill non-pest species such as beetles and moths, and these non-pest insects are important food for birds and bats. Thus, electrocution traps may actually reduce the number of birds that visit your backyard!

Home owners should use an integrated approach to control mosquito populations. To help reduce the number of mosquitoes, you should remove water receptacles, apply insect repellent to yourself, and even build houses for bats and birds as a biological control. Insect-eating bats and birds (e.g., purple martins) may drastically reduce the number of mosquitoes around your home, and they are certainly of educational and aesthetic value!

Several different herbs can also be used to ward off mosquitoes. Pennyroyal and tansey are known to keep away mosquitoes. Historically, sprigs of tansey were placed by pioneers in windows of their log cabins for this purpose. Without screens for windows, sleeping inside one's house was most likely a miserable experience! People in some countries even keep pigs inside their homes to keep the hungry mosquitoes happily fed during the night. Apparently, mosquitoes prefer pigs to humans. Anybody willing to sleep with a pig in their house?

Mosquitoes are notorious carriers of malaria, yellow fever, dengue fever, and encephalitis. Although malaria, yellow fever, and dengue fever do not normally occur in the U.S., some mosquitoes carry Eastern and Western strains of encephalitis (notably the Asian tiger mosquito, *Aedes albopictus*). However, the chance of humans acquiring encephalitis is remote. Both strains primarily infect birds, occasionally horses, and in rare cases, humans. In 1991, 150 horses and 5 humans contracted eastern equine encephalitis in the state of Florida (as reported by the Florida Department of Agriculture and Consumer Services). Vaccinations are available for horses to prevent them from contracting the disease.

Fun Things to Do with Mosquitoes

What is it that attracts female mosquitoes to certain people? Some people notoriously have "sweeter blood" than other people. I know that when I am in a crowd of people, I am the first one to be bitten. Researchers believe that odor, temperature, carbon dioxide emission, and color all play a role in attracting mosquitoes. Ever wonder what it is about yourself that attracts mosquitoes the most? Well, you can design a few scientific experiments.

First, build a small cage for your mosquitoes, and place a trap door at the bottom. The frame of the cage can be made from any material, but the sides should consist of a fine netting.

Now, let's obtain some mosquitoes. The easiest way to do this is to set out, in a shady place, a small plastic butter or yogurt container with some leaf litter and 3 to 5 inches of water. After three or four days, check the container for mosquito larvae. If you see some, place the container inside your cage and wait for them to hatch. To speed the process of hatching, you can feed the larvae Tetratin® "E" baby fish food.

You can even do some experiments with the larvae. Put a light at one end of the cage. Which way do the larvae go? Do they respond to you touching the edge of the container? If so, why did they respond to your actions? If you time it just right, you can even watch the adults hatch out!

Now you can do a variety of experiments on female mosquitoes. (Remember, they are the ones that bite!) First, separate the females from the males (males have feathery antennae). Then observe which side of the cage the females normally rest on. These observations are important because the mosquitoes may actually prefer one side of the cage before you even do any experiments. You can greatly equalize preferences by placing the cage in a large cardboard box. There are many other factors which may influence mosquito activity (e.g., time of day, temperature of room, light), so make sure you conduct your control experiments (observations without the test material) and actual experiments in the same conditions.

Okay, let's conduct some experiments! To test the effect of temperature, fill up two balloons—one with with warm water and one with cold. Place the balloons on opposite sides of the cage (make sure they touch the screen), and observe which balloon attracts the most mosquitoes during fifteen minutes. What temperature seems to attract the most female mosquitoes? Why? Try this test on males. Do they respond differently?

You can also test the odor of your friends and family. Have a person rub a blown-up balloon (or even marbles or cloth), and tape it to one side of the cage; tape a clean balloon to the other side and record the number of mosquitoes that land on each balloon. Compare balloons rubbed by different people. If the mosquitoes did show preferences, what made them choose different people? What do people produce that attracts mosquitoes? Why is it important for mosquitoes to smell?

The color of the balloon may be important, so test different balloon colors. Light may also play a role, so compare a dark side of the cage to a light side. Test for attraction to carbon dioxide by breathing heavily into a cloth, and placing it on one side of the cage. (Remember to place another clean cloth on the other side.) Are females attracted to the carbon dioxide cloth? What about males?

You can play around with a number of different combinations to find the one that most attracts mosquitoes. Furthermore, you can test many substances that you think may repel mosquitoes. You might even discover a new homemade insect repellent mixture. Try different types of herbs. Why do you think mosquitoes are repelled by certain substances?

Design other experiments, such as in what type of water do female mosquitoes prefer to lay their eggs in (e.g., fresh vs. salty; rainwater vs. tap water)? Do females prefer different colored containers? Perform some tests on male "hearing" capabilities. If you have some tuning forks or a guitar, strike them and see which frequencies attract males.

Common Mosquitoes Hit by Cars and Trucks

☐ YELLOW FEVER MOSQUITO (*Aedes aegypti*)

Local distribution:

These mosquitoes can be encountered on roads primarily in South Florida during the summer, especially at night after heavy rains.

Eggs and larvae:

Oval-shaped eggs are normally deposited along the sides of human-made containers (i.e., tires) near the water line. Eggs can remain viable for several months without water. Larvae hang at an angle from the surface of the water and mature within seven days.

Adults:

Adults do not travel more than 100 yards from their birth site. They feed mostly during the day and sometimes at night. They live approximately ten weeks.

Interesting facts:

The yellow fever mosquito is becoming relatively rare in South Florida; apparently it is being driven out by the Asian tiger mosquito (*Aedes albopictus*). Researchers have several hypotheses about why the yellow fever mosquito is disappearing. One hypothesis states that Asian tiger larvae are much better competitors for food than the yellow fever larvae. Other researchers propose that when Asian tiger males mate with yellow fever females (which they sometimes do), the female will never again mate with a male of her own species. Because her eggs are not successfully fertilized by the Asian tiger male, no young are produced. Also, some researchers have found parasites on Asian tiger larvae that are much more harmful to yellow fever larvae than to the Asian tiger larvae. Thus, when the two species of larvae occur in the same water container, most of the yellow fever larvae are killed, whereas most of the Asian tiger larvae survive!

☐ **COMMON NORTHERN HOUSE MOSQUITO**
(*Culex pipiens pipiens*) **and**

☐ **SOUTHERN HOUSE MOSQUITO**
(*Culex pipiens quinquefasciatus*)

Local distribution:

These mosquitoes can be encountered on most roads during warm months at dusk.

Eggs and larvae:

Eggs are normally deposited in discarded containers, bird baths, and street drains, where the water is foul and contains abundant algae.

Found in groups or "rafts," eggs float on top of the water. Larvae hang at an angle from the surface of the water, and can reach the adult stage within two to three weeks.

Adults:

Adults can travel up to several miles from their birth site and feed at night. They live twelve to fourteen weeks and can transmit bird malaria.

Interesting facts:

The common house mosquito is a notorious pest on people's porches. You can easily identify them by their resting posture; they hold their bodies almost parallel to the surface.

☐ MALARIA MOSQUITOES (Genus: *Anopheles*)

Local distribution:

These mosquitoes can be encountered on most roads during the summer, especially at dusk.

Eggs and larvae:

Eggs are normally deposited in lakes, ponds, and swamps. The eggs occur separately, are boat-shaped, and have small air-floats attached to the sides. Larvae rest parallel to the surface of the water and become adults within two weeks.

Adults:

Adults can travel up to several miles from their birth site. They feed at night and live approximately two to three weeks. Some species can transmit human malaria, (although malaria is generally absent in North America.)

Interesting facts:

Several species of malaria mosquitoes are found throughout North America. You can recognize them by their resting posture. They hold their bodies at a 45 degree angle to a surface. Also, their wings appear to be spotted. The larvae rest parallel to the water surface because they lack a breathing tube.

☐ SALT-MARSH MOSQUITOES
(*Aedes sollicitans* and *taeniorhynchus*)

Local distribution:

These mosquitoes can be encountered on most coastal roads (excluding the Northwest) during the summer. You can hit quite a few of these mosquitoes near the coast or any salt marsh, especially after heavy rains.

Eggs and larvae:

Eggs are located in the sod of dense grass at the edge of salt marshes. Eggs remain viable from one to several years if no water is present. Larvae hang at an angle from the surface of the water, and reach the adult stage within seven to nine days.

Adults:

Adults have been known to travel as far as twenty-five miles from their birth sites. They feed both during the day and night, and they live for about a month.

Interesting facts:

In Florida, *A. sollicitans* is very abundant along the coast in the north, and *A. taeniorhynchus* in the south. These two mosquitoes are more plentiful than any other species of mosquito in this state. In some parts of Florida, 113 million eggs per acre have been estimated. Boy!...Watch out when it floods!

☐ ASIAN TIGER MOSQUITO (*Aedes albopictus*)

Local distribution:

These mosquitoes can be encountered on most roads in the Southeast during the summer, especially at dusk after heavy rains.

Eggs and larvae:

Oval-shaped eggs are normally deposited along the sides of human-made containers (i.e. tires) near the water line. Eggs can remain viable for several months without water. Larvae hang at an angle from the surface of the water and mature within seven days.

Adults:

Adults do not travel more than 100 yards from their birth sites, feeding during the day and at night. Adults can transmit yellow fever, dengue fever, and encephalitis. (They live about ten weeks.)

Interesting facts:

Females of this species primarily feed on humans and are much more aggressive than *A. aegypti*. They are thought to have been transported from Asia to the U.S. in tires. Asian tiger mosquitoes may be displacing yellow fever mosquitoes. Researchers have some hypotheses about why yellow fever mosquitoes are disappearing (see page 89), but it is still being debated. (Hmm . . . sounds like a potential research opportunity if anyone is motivated!)

☐ GLADES MOSQUITOES (Genus: *Psorophora*)

Local distribution:

During warm months, Psorophoran mosquitoes can be encountered in most regions of the U.S. (except the Northwest). You can hit quite a few of these mosquitoes on roads crossing the Florida Everglades.

Eggs and larvae:

Eggs are deposited near sites that become filled with water. Eggs can remain viable up to a year. Larvae can reach the adult stage within five days.

Adults:

Adults can travel up to ten miles from their breeding sites. They live about one to two weeks. They feed mostly at night, but sometimes during the day.

Interesting facts:

This mosquito is notorious to those who travel within the boundaries of the Everglades. Campers have told me glade mosquitoes bite right through clothing! One species, *P. ciliata*, can be as large as 10 mm and has been reported to kill cattle (so they say). Larvae of *P. ciliata* are known to feed on other species of mosquito larvae.

☐ MANSONIA MOSQUITOES (Genus: *Mansonia*)

Local distribution:

These mosquitoes can be encountered on most roads in the Southeast during the summer at dusk.

Eggs and larvae:

Eggs are deposited near aquatic plants and occur as rafts similar to *Culex*. Larvae take several months to develop into adults.

Adults:

Adults can travel up to five miles from their breeding sites and feed mostly at dusk. Adults can transmit encephalitis and heart worms to dogs.

Interesting facts:

The larval stage for this mosquito is quite long, and it remains beneath the water, obtaining oxygen from the cells of aquatic plants. Mansonia larvae have specially adapted pointed siphons (on the tip of the abdomen), which they insert into plant cells.

· MUSCID FLIES ·

ORDER: DIPTERA
FAMILY: MUSCIDAE

Ahh! . . . These flies are a familiar sight in everybody's home. Their habit of feeding on excrement and decaying matter makes these insects a most unwelcome visitor. Maggots, or fly larvae, are seen wherever rotting organic matter is found. In the past, scientists were amazed that these maggots spontaneously emerged when a piece of food was left out in the open. They thought these worm-like creatures magically formed from substances in the food! Today we know adult flies lay their eggs on the food.

There are over 700 species in this family, with both biting and non-biting varieties. By far the most abundant fly, the house fly *Musca domestica*, is a common nonbiting pest in households. A common belief about this fly is that it "throws up" every time it lands on you. Well, this house fly does regurgitate fluid in order to dissolve dry food items, but it will not vomit every time it lands on you . . . unless of course, you have some dry food particles on your skin that it wants to eat.

One species, the stable fly (*Stomoxys calcitrans*), looks just like a house fly, but differs in a most important way—it bites! Confusion between the stable and house fly have led many people to think that house flies will bite when given the chance. Another unusual thing about stable flies is that both sexes bite! They feed on the blood of humans, livestock, and pets. So the next time you are bitten by what looks like a house fly . . . remember, it's the stable fly!

Did you know house flies spit on their food before they eat it?!

That's gross.

Natural Life History of Muscid Flies

Adults are quite numerous during the summer months and are continuously mating and laying eggs. A male copulates with a female by tackling her in the air. The pair usually tumbles to the ground in what looks like a confused heap. There, the male inseminates the female. The whole drama takes only a few seconds.

Containing fertilized eggs, the female chooses a suitable pile of rotting organic matter and proceeds to lay a batch of eggs, which number from 100 to 150. Females can lay from four to six batches in their lifetimes. Eggs are clumped together, and each egg is white, a little under 1 mm in length, and has two lines running down the length of the egg. Eggs hatch within eight to twelve hours, and larvae molt two times before pupating. The whole process, from egg to adult, takes about eight or ten days, depending on the temperature.

To control muscid flies, the best thing you can do is remove all possible decaying matter around your house. In other words, keep tight lids on all garbage cans and remove pet or animal feces.

Fun Things to Do with Muscid Flies

As a kid, I used to feed house flies to my pet toad and two anole lizards (named Sinbad and Lizzy). If you have a toad or a lizard, watch how each animal tracks down a fly and catches it! Immobilize a fly. Can your toad see a fly that is not moving?

House flies can be trapped if you are quick with your hand (I actually became quite good at this), or they can be caught with small nets. You can find house flies by hanging around fresh horse manure, or by setting out any rotting food and waiting for them to arrive. Time how long it takes for the flies to discover the food that you set out for them. How do adult flies detect rotting material so quickly?

If you would like to raise a few muscid flies, it is quite easy. Place at least six flies in a cage that contains some rotting food scraps (e.g., fruits and vegetables). Within a few days, you will observe a bunch of larvae crawling around, happily munching on your food scraps. Once they pupate, take the pupae and place them in a dry dish inside the cage. Watch these pupae carefully; you might be able to see them hatch. Pretty soon, you will have lots of flies! These flies can be used to feed your pet lizards or toads.

Common House and Stable Flies Hit by Cars and Trucks

☐ **COMMON HOUSE FLY (*Musca domestica*) and**

☐ **STABLE FLY (*Stomoxys calcitrans*)**

Local distribution:

These flies are encountered on most roads throughout the year during the day.

Eggs and larvae:

Eggs and larvae are found in dung and rotting organic matter.

Adults:

Adults are quite common indoors.

·SOLDIER FLIES·

ORDER: DIPTERA
FAMILY: STRATIOMYIDAE

These flies are rather large (6 to 18 mm in length), dark-colored, and rather inconspicuous. Soldier flies apparently acquired this name because of their sometimes metallic colorations and spike-like hairs on their thoraxes. There are over 250 North American species.

Soldier flies are primarily nonbiting flower feeders that are seen most of the time at rest. (Maybe they should have been called "hippie flies.") When flying, the sometimes flashy-colored abdomens are quite conspicuous, but when at rest on vegetation, the wings cover the flashy parts which renders them quite invisible. So, why do you think they have flashy colors? Perhaps color is used for mating purposes and individuals of different species recognize each other by displaying particular color patterns.

Where have all the soldier flies gone?, gone to flowers every one...

Natural Life History of Soldier Flies

Not much is known about the biology of soldier flies. Most larvae are aquatic, breathing air from the surface with siphons; others live in decaying vegetable and animal matter. Adults are thought to feed primarily on flower nectar and pollen.

Fun Things to Do with Soldier Flies

Not much is known about the biology of soldier flies. These flies are sort of wasp-like (but with only two wings) and can be found during the spring and summer around various flowers. Watching them in their natural surroundings will provide much new information. When are they most active? Do males swarm? Where do females oviposit eggs? Which flowers do they prefer to feed on?

Catch a few of these flies and rear them in a cage. Take careful notes on their behavior and life cycle. How do they feed on flowers? Will they feed on other organic matter (e.g., sugar)? How long do the adults live? What is the duration of the larval stage? What do the pupae look like?

Common Soldier Flies Hit by Cars and Trucks

☐ **COMMON SOLDIER FLIES (Family: Stratiomyidae)**

Local distribution:

These insects are on most roads during the day throughout the spring and summer.

Eggs and larvae:

Eggs and larvae are found mostly in water.

Adults:

Adults are quite common outdoors.

COLLECTING AND MOUNTING INSECTS

How you collect insects is up to you. You can use a fine mesh net, paper bags, jars, and even your hands to catch them. If, however, you want to collect those insects that careen off the front of your windshield, you'll need wire mesh carcass catcher just above the top of your windshield. The easiest way to make one is to find some aluminum screening and enough stiff wire to traverse the top of your car twice. Attach the aluminum screen to one of the wires by rolling it around the wire, and then stretch the mesh across to the other wire. Leave about 6 inches of mesh between the two wires and shape the mesh into a cup shape in order to trap the insects. Now place your "net" across the top of your car near the windshield and bend the wires through the passenger's and driver's door. (Note: the doors should be able to close fairly easily without bending the trim on your car.) You should have a continuous band of mesh across the top of your car. Depending on the slope of your windshield, you will have to adjust the position of your insect net in order to trap insects flying up over the top of your car.

If you have a live insect for your collection, you need to kill it without damaging the specimen. You can freeze insects or construct a "killing bottle" (which is much faster). Bottles should be screw-capped or corked, and you should have several sizes of bottles for various sizes of insects. Bottles used for Lepidopterans (butterflies and moths) should be kept separate, because the scales will come off and adhere to other insects. There are many different types of killing agents, but I recommend using ethyl acetate because it is the least dangerous toxin to humans. However, you should not breathe this in excess—it will make you sick! You can find ethyl acetate in fingernail polish remover (non-acetone) at any store. To make the killing bottle, place some cotton on the bottom of the bottle and add a couple of drops of fingernail polish remover. Promptly place some cardboard or a screen over the top of the cotton and screw on the lid to prevent fumes from escaping. The barrier between the insect and the cotton prevents the insect from getting tangled up in it. All jars should be kept dry and conspicuously labeled "Poison!"

All insects should be mounted as soon as possible before they become brittle. Pinning is the best way to preserve specimens. Specially-made insect pins should be used because they are longer and do not rust. Pin sizes range from 00 to 7; use sizes 2 to 4 for general use. If you cannot find these insect pins, you can use longer store-bought pins.

Insects should be pinned vertically through the dorsal (top) side of the insect. For butterflies and moths, the pins should go through the thorax between the base of the front wings. Flies and wasps should be pinned just right of the middle of the thorax. Beetles, cockroaches, and large grasshoppers are pinned halfway down the body, just right of the midline. You can mount very small insects on small, triangular pieces of white cardboard. The base of the cardboard is stuck with a pin and an insect is glued to the end of the triangle.

All specimens should be mounted at a uniform height (25 mm) above the cardboard. Pins can be stuck into mounting boards made of cork, balsa wood, Styrofoam, or cardboard. Each pinned insect should always have a small label at the bottom with the date and location of the insects capture. You also can provide a separate label with the scientific name for each specimen. Mounting boards are placed in dust-proof boxes, such as cigar boxes. To keep other insects from eating your collection (e.g., cockroaches), place a few moth balls in your box (but do not place moth balls too close to colorful insects or they will lose their color).

With butterflies and moths, you need to spread the wings so they will stay horizontal once pinned. If you pinned them without spreading the wings, the wings will curl up and you cannot view them. To spread the wings, turn the insect upside down on a flat, pinnable surface, and hold the wings down on both sides with two thin strips of cardboard. Pin the wings on each side in the following manner: first, gently move the front wings up, one at a time, and place pins through the cardboard strips, close to the wings. Now move the hind wings down and pin them in similar fashion as before. Leave the butterfly or moth in this position until the wings are stiff. Afterward, you can remove the strips of cardboard and turn the butterfly over to mount it.

GAMES YOU CAN PLAY IN THE CAR

This section contains games (about insects) to occupy your time while driving down the road. Have fun!

Don't Spell Wasp!

This game can be played by two to six people. The object of this game is not to spell a word in its entirety. One person starts by saying any letter he or she wants, but this person must be thinking of the name of an insect or anything remotely related to insects (e.g., body parts, behavior, or habitats) that starts with this letter. Then, the next person continues by saying a second letter, but now these two letters cannot spell a word, any word (e.g., to or at). Now this person also must be thinking of any type of insect or anything related to insects (proper names and places do not count) that starts with these two letters, but not necessarily the same thing as what the previous person was thinking.

If you cannot think of any letter that follows the sequence of letters already stated, you can trick the next person by saying any letter that seems to fit. At anytime, though, the next person can challenge you, and then you must produce the word. If you cannot, then you get the first letter W in the word wasp. You also can get a letter in the word wasp if you accidentally spell a word or you cannot continue on with the next letter. The person who loses each round begins the next round with a new letter. Every person that spells wasp drops out of the game, and the last person not to spell wasp wins the game.

My Side–Your Side

Divide the front windshield into halves or quarters, depending on the number of players. The object of this game is to count the number of insects that hit your portion of the windshield during the trip (bird doo-doo does not count). The person with the most splats wins! . . . Or, the one with the least number of splats wins. This game is especially exciting in May and September (i.e., lovebug season).

Collection Inspection

Yes, this game involves actually collecting whole insects. Each person should be equipped with some type of net. Stick the net out the window and see how many different types of insects you can catch (Be careful! Use a small net and do not stick it out too far, especially with other cars in the vicinity). You will catch a lot of insects in the early morning and at night. Also, at different rest stops, you can collect a variety of insects—especially when you travel through several states. Once you have caught some insects, try and see if you can identify them, at least to their respective order or family. Be sure to bring several jars in which to place them.

Hangfly

Played just like hangman . . . except you draw a fly: head, thorax, abdomen, a pair of wings, three pairs of legs, and a pair of eyes. Further, all words used are restricted to insects or anything related to insects.

I hate it when you're always on MY side!

Insect Art

Place a clear piece of saran wrap across the front of your windshield before you head on down the road (make sure it extends below the surface of your hood or it will just blow off). At the end of your trip, carefully peel the saran wrap off your windshield and you will have quite a collection of bug splats. Art at its finest!

I prefer Collection Inspection...less painful.

BIRDS, INSECTS,
AND AUTOMOBILES

D riving down the road, have you ever noticed birds (such as doves, blackbirds, sparrows, and starlings) just walking along the side of the road pecking at something on the ground? Guess what? They are eating all those insects that were unfortunate enough to hit our cars and fall on the side of the road! Yes, our speeding vehicles sometimes supply a feast of insect bodies for a few of our feathered friends. Be especially careful when driving by mourning doves, these birds tend to wait until you are just upon them before taking flight.

In fact, it has long been observed that sparrows will investigate the grills of parked cars and pick off the remains of insects. While in the Badlands National Park in South Dakota, I stopped at a parking area to hike the Cliff Shelf Nature Trail and, on the way back, I noticed a black-billed magpie hopping from one car bumper to another, calmly eating the insects despite the melee of tourists snapping pictures and pointing excitedly at it. This bird was very meticulous, eyeing each part of the bumper and removing what seemed to be only the freshest insect splat. I wager if you were to visit the Cliff Shelf Nature Trail today, you could also observe the same black-billed magpie (or others like it) cleaning the front of your car's bumper!

· REFERENCES ·

Below, I have listed those books and journals that were used as sources of information for this book. I have also added some books that I thought were of interest.

THE INSECTS

ANTS

Ordish, G. (1978). *The Year of the Ant*. New York: Charles Scribner Sons.

Sudd, J. H. (1967). *An Introduction to the Behavior of Ants*. New York: St. Martin's Press.

BEES

Gould, J. L. and C. G. Gould (1988). *The Honey Bee*. New York: Scientific American Library.

BEETLES

Buschman, L. L. (1977). "Biology and Bioluminescence of Selected Fireflies in Three Genera: *Pyractomena, Photinus and Photuris* (Coleoptera: Lampyridae)." M.S. Thesis, University of Florida.

Krysan, J. L. and T. A. Miller (1986). *Methods for the Study of the Pest Diabrotica*. New York: Springer-Verlag.

BUTTERFLIES

Brewer, J. and D. Winter (1986). *Butterflies and Moths*. New York: Prentice Hall Press.

Gerberg, E. J. and R. H. Arnett, Jr. (1989). *Florida Butterflies*. Baltimore, Maryland: Natural Science Publications.

Tyler, H. A. (1975). *The Swallowtail Butterflies of North America*. Healdsburg, CA: Naturegraph Publishers.

Urquhart, F. A. (1987). *The Monarch Butterfly: International Traveler* (232 ed.). Chicago: Nelson-Hall.

CADDISFLIES

Betten, C. (1934). *The Caddisflies or Trichoptera of New York State*. Albany, NY: The University of the State of New York.

CICADAS

Myers, J. G. (1929). *Insect Singers*. London: George Routledge and Sons, Ltd.

COCKROACHES

Cornwell, P. B. (1968). *The Cockroach: A Laboratory Insect and an Industrial Pest*. London: Hutchinson & Company Ltd.

Hostetler, Mark. (1992). "Behavioral and Physiological Resistance to Pesticides in the German Cockroach (*Blatella germanica*): An Experimental Reevaluation. M.S. Thesis, University of Florida.

CRANEFLIES

Sullivan, R. T. (1981). "Mating Behavior of Craneflies (Diptera: Tipulidae)." M.S. Thesis, University of Florida.

DRAGONFLIES

Corbert, P. S., C. Longfield, and N. W. Moore (1960). *Dragonflies*. London: Collins Clear-Type Press.

Dunkle, S. W. (1989). *Dragonflies of the Florida Peninsula, Bermuda, and the Bahamas*. Gainesville, FL: Scientific Publishers.

Miller, P. L. (1987). *Dragonflies*. New York: Cambridge University Press.

FLIES

Blanton, F. S. and W. W. Wirth (1979). *Arthropods of Florida and Neighboring Land Areas, Volume 10, The Sand Flies (Culicoides) of Florida*. Gainesville, FL: Florida Department of Agricultural and Consumer Services, Division of Plant Industry.

Curran, C. H. (1934). *The Families and Genera of North American Diptera*. New York: The Ballou Press.

Hewitt, C. G. (1914). *The House Fly*. Cambridge, England: Cambridge University Press.

Oldroyd, H. (1964). *The Natural History of Flies*. New York, NY: W. W. Norton & Company, Inc.

HOVERFLIES

Gilbert, F. S. (1986). *Hoverflies*. New York: Cambridge University Press.

LACEWINGS

Hydorn, S. B. (1971). "Food Preferences of Chrysopa rufilabris (Burmeister) in North Central Florida." M.S. Thesis, University of Florida.

LOVEBUGS

Callahan, P. S. and H. A. Denmark (1973). *Attraction of the "Lovebug,"* Plecia nearctica *(Diptera: Bibionidae)*. Florida Entomol.: 59(2): 191-194.

MOLE CRICKETS

Forrest, T. G. (1981). "Acoustic Behavior, Phonotaxi, and Mate Choice in Two Species of Mole Crickets (Gryllotalpidae: Scapteriscus)." M.S. Thesis, University of Florida.

Saller, R. I., J. A. Reinert, D. Boucias, P. Busey, R. L. Kepner, T. G. Forrest, W. G. Hudson, and T. J. Walker (1984). *"Mole Crickets in Florida,"* in T. J. Walker (Ed.), *Florida Agricultural Experimental Station Bulletin* (pp. 36). Gainesville, FL: Institute of Food and Agricultural Sciences.

MOSQUITOES

Bates, M. (1949). *The Natural History of Mosquitoes*. New York: The Macmillan Company.

Horsfall, W. R. (1972). *Mosquitoes, Their Bionomics and Relation to Disease*. New York: Hafner Publishing Company.

Mitchell, E. G. (1907). *Mosquito Life*. New York, NY: The Knickerbocker Press.

Snow, K. R. (1990). *Mosquitoes*. Slough, England: Richmond Publishing Co. Ltd.

MOTHS

Covel, C. V., Jr. (1984). *A Field Guide to the Moths of Eastern North America*. Boston: Houghton Mifflin.

Ford, E. B. (1955). *Moths*. London: Collins Clear-Type Press.

CHILDREN'S PICTURE BOOKS

Brouillette, J. (1963). *Insects*. Chicago: Follet Publishing Co.

Brown, M. (1985). *Hand Rhymes*. New York: E. P. Dutton.

Carle, E. (1977). *The Grouchy Ladybug*. New York: T. Y. Crowell Co.

Carle, E. (1981). *The Very Hungry Caterpillar*. New York: Philomel Books.

Conklin, G. (1968). *Lucky Ladybugs*. New York: Holiday House.

Dorros, A. (1987). *Ant Cities*. New York: Harper & Row Publishers.

Fisher-Nagel, H. and A. (1987). *Life of the Butterfly*. Minneapolis: Carolrhoda Books, Inc.

Fleischman, Paul. (1988). *Joyful Noise: Poems for Two Voices*. USA: Harper Trophy.

Granseth, S. and D. McMillen (1989). *Bugs, Bugs, Bugs*. Des Moines: Meredith Corporation.

Ipcar, D. (1975). *Bug City*. New York: Holiday House.

Knight, D. C. (1967). *Let's Find Out About Insects*. New York: Franklin Watts Inc.

Lepthien, E. (1989). *Monarch Butterflies*. Chicago: Childrens Press.

McGavin, G. (1989). *Bugs*. New York: The Bookwright Press.

McGavin, G. (1989). *Discovering Bugs*. New York: The Bookwright Press.

Myrick, M. (1968). *Ants are Fun*. New York: Harper & Row Publishers.

O'Hagan, C. (1980). *It's Easy to have a Caterpillar Visit You*. New York: Lothrop, Lee & Shepard Books.

Parker Winslow, N. and J. Richards Wright (1987). *Bugs*. New York: Greenwillow Books.

Porter, K. (1986). *Butterflies and Moths*. New York: The Bookwright Press.

Reidel, M. (1981). *From Egg to Butterfly*. Minneapolis: Carolrhoda Books, Inc.

Roels, L. (1969). *The Bee*. New York: Grosset & Dunlap.

Selsam, M. and R. Goor (1981). *Backyard Insects*. New York: Four Winds Press.

Stevens, C. (1961). *Catch a Cricket*. Reading, Massachusetts: Addison-Wesley Publishing Co.

Stevens, C. (1978). *Insect Pets: Catching and Caring for Them*. New York: Greenwillow Books.

Van Allsburg, C. (1988). *Two Bad Ants*. Boston: Houghton Mifflin.

GENERAL READING

Arnett, R. H., Jr. (1993). *American Insects: A Handbook of the Insects of America North of Mexico*. Gainesville, FL: The Sandhill Crane Press, Inc.

Borror, J. B., D. M. Delong and C. A. Triplehorn (1981). *An Introduction to the Study of Insects* (5 ed.). New York, N Y: Saunders College Publishing.

Botha, C., S. Cerulean, and D. Legare. *Planting a Refuge for Wildlife.* Florida: General Florida Game and Fresh Water Fish Commission Nongame Wildlife Program, and United States Department of Agriculture Soil Conservation Service.

Chapman, R. F. (1982). *The Insects: Structure and Function.* Cambridge, Massachusetts: Harvard University Press.

Cornell, J. (1988). *Sharing the Joy of Nature.* Nevada City, CA: Dawn Publishing.

Feinsinger, P. and M. Minno (1990). *Handbook to schoolyard plants and animals of North Central Florida.* Gainesville, FL: The Nongame Wildlife Program, Florida Game and Fresh Water Fish Commission.

Garber, S. D. (1987). *The Urban Naturalist.* New York, NY: John Wiley & Sons, Inc.

Milne, L. J. and M. Milne (1980). *The Audubon Society Field Guide to North American Insects and Spiders.* New York: Knopf.

Mitchell, J. H. (1985). *A Field Guide to Your Own Backyard.* New York: Norton.

Platt, Rutherford H., R.A. Rowntree, and P.C. Muick (1994). *The Ecological City: Preserving and Restoring Biodiversity.* Amherst, MA: University of Massachusetts Press.

Pyle, R. M. (1981). *The Audubon Society Field Guide to North American Butterflies.* New York: Knopf.

Stokes, D. W. (1983). *A Guide to Observing Insect Lives.* Boston: Little, Brown.

White, R. E. (1970). *A Field Guide to the Insects of America North of Mexico.* Boston: Houghton Mifflin.

William, H. J. (1977). *Windowsill Ecology.* Emmaus, PA: Rodale.

Wilson, E. O. (1972). *The Insect Societies.* Cambridge, MA: Belknap Press of Harvard University Press.

· GLOSSARY ·

abdomen The end portion of an insect that contains the digestive system.

alate A flying ant.

bioluminescent Emission of light by living organisms.

control experiment An experiment made to verify the results of another experiment(s) using the same condition except for one factor or variable.

cryptic The method of concealing oneself from predators; camouflage.

deciduous In plants, those characteristics of losing leaves once a year.

diapause In insects, a period of suspended development during which physiological activity is very low.

eye spot A coloration on the wings of some insects that resembles an eye.

fauna The animals of a particular place or time.

flora The plants of a particular place or time.

gall An abnormal growth that forms on the leaves and stems of plants, caused by insects.

groom To clean oneself.

larva The worm-like stage of a newly hatched insect, before it becomes an adult.

mandibles The mouthparts of an insect that are used for seizing and biting food.

metamorphosis In insects, the process of going through several distinct stages of growth (egg: larva: pupa: adult).

microhabitat A habitat, usually within a small area, containing a small number of insects.

molt To shed feathers, skin, hair, shell, antlers, or other growths before new growth occurs.

nocturnal A description of organisms that are active at night.

organic debris Scraps of material that are derived from living organisms, such as pieces of leaves.

oviposit To deposit or lay eggs.

papillae Small projections on certain parts of an insect's body that contain receptors for touch, taste, or smell.

pest A term that refers to any insect that is injurious in some way to humans.

pheromone Any of various chemicals secreted by an animal that influence specific patterns of behavior by other members of the same species.

predator An animal that eats other animals.

prey An animal that is hunted or caught for food.

proboscis The tubelike mouth part of some insects (e.g., flies and mosquitoes) that is used for sucking or piercing.

protozoan Any single-celled microscopic organism in the phylum Protozoa.

pupa The inactive stage of many insects that follows the larval stage.

substrate A surface on which a plant or animal grows or is attached.

thorax The middle region (behind the head) of an insect.

UV light Ultraviolet light, invisible to the human eye.

ultrasonic Having to do with sound waves beyond the range of human hearing.

ventral The lower surface of the body of an animal.

INDEX

A

Acetone, insect poison, 46

Aedes aegypti. See Mosquitoes, yellow fever

Aedes albopictus. See Asian tiger mosquitoes

Aedes canadensis. See Mosquitoes

Aedes sollicitans. See Mosquitoes, salt-marsh

Aedes taeniorhynchus. See Mosquitoes, salt-marsh

Agrypinia vestita. See Caddisflies

Alates, 1, 2, 5

Amber, 1

American cockroach, 37

Anax junius. See Green darner

Anopheles. See Mosquitoes, malaria

Antlions, **Plate II**, 6–8

    cultivation, 7

Ants, 1–5

    activities, 1

    and aphids, 2

    carpenter, 4

    cultivation, 7

    fire, **Plate I**, 4

    pheromones, 2

    scent trail, 2

    supplanting nests, 3

    types, 1

Aphids, and ants, 2

Apis mellifera. See Honey bees

Asian cockroach, 36

Asian tiger mosquitoes, 86, 90

B

Banded cucumber beetle, 40, 42

Basilarchia archippus. See Viceroy butterfly

Bat, brown, 83

Battus philenor. See Pipevine swallowtail butterfly

Beetles

    cucumber, 41–42

    pheromones, 41

Bioluminescence, 49

Biston betularae. See Pepper moth

Biting midges, 9–10

Black flies, **Plate IV**, 11–13

    diseases carried by, 11

Blattella asahinia. See Asian cockroach

Blood meal, 84

Brachynemurus spp. *See* Antlions

Butterflies, 14-24
    cultivation, 18
    defense mechanism, 16
    pheromones, 17
    pollination, 17
    repellent larvae, 16
    tiger swallowtail, **Plate V**

C

Caddisflies, **Plate VI**, 25-26
    cultivation, 26
Camouflage
    caterpillars, 16
    lacewings, 71
    tiger swallowtail butterfly, 122
Camponotus. See Carpenter ants
Cankerworms, 20
Car games, 101-102
Carpenter ants, 4
Caterpillars, 16
    camouflage, 16
    cultivation, 18
    defense mechanism, 16
Celithemis eponina. See Dragonflies
Celtis laevigata. See Sugarberry (tree)
Ceratopogonidae. See Midges, biting
Cerci, 79
Chironomidae. See Midges
Choristoneura fumiferana. See Spruce budworm

Chrysalis, 16
Chrysopa oculata. See Lacewings
Chrysopa rufilabris. See Lacewings
Chrysopa spp. *See* Lacewings
Chrysops. See Deer flies
Cicadas, **Plate VII**, 27-30
    cultivation, 28
    in fables, 27
    seventeen year, 27
    sound, 27
Citrus white flies, 71
Cockroaches, 31-37
    allergy to, 32
    American, **Plate VIII**
    control of, 34
    cultivation, 35
    defense mechanism, 33, 35
    diseases carried by, 32
    pheromones, 33
    reduction of, 34
Cocoon, 16
Collecting insects, 99-100
Control methods
    cockroaches, 34
    fire ants, 5
    mole crickets, 81
    mosquitoes, 86
    muscid flies, 95
Corn earworm, 20
Corn rootworm, 40
Crambus. See Moths

E

Eastern tiger swallowtail, 22
Electrocution traps, 86
Encephalitis, 86
Eristalis tenax. See Drone flies
Erythemis simplicicollis. See
  Pondhawk
Ethyl acetate, 99
Eurycotis floridana. See
  Palmetto bug

F

Fire ants, **Plate I**, 4, 5
  control of, 5
Fireflies, **Plate XII**, 49–52
  cultivation, 50
Flies
  black, **Plate IV**, 11–13
  butter, 14–24
  caddis, **Plate VI**, 25–26
  citrus white flies, 71
  crane, **Plate IX**
  damsel, 43
  deer, **Plate XV**, 61–62
  dragon, **Plate XI**, 43–48
  drone, 64
  fire, **Plate XII**, 49–52
  green darner, 47
  horse, **Plate XV**, 61–62
  house, 94, 96
  hover, **Plate XVI**, 63–67

muscid, **Plate XXIII**, 94–96
sand, 9
soldier, **Plate XXIV**, 97–98
stable, 94, 96
syrphus, 66
volucella, 66
Formaldehyde, 74
Formic acid, 4
Formica fusca. See Ants
Formica rufa. See Ants
Frisch, Karl von, 56

G

Galleria mellonella, 21
Galls, 68
Geckos, 34
Geometer moths, 19
Geometridae. See Geometer
  moths
Glyptotendipes paripes. See
  Midges
Grapholitha molesta. See
  Oriental fruit moth
Grasshoppers, 53–55
  American, **Plate XIII**, 53
Grass moths, 20
Gravid, 82
Green darner, 47

H

Hangfly (game), 102
Heliothis zea. See Corn
  earworm

Heptaldehyde, 74

Heraclides cresphontes. See
   Tiger swallowtail caterpillar

Heraclides glaucus. See Eastern
   tiger swallowtail butterfly

Heraclides rutulus. See Western
   tiger swallowtail butterfly

Hermetia illucens. See Soldier
   flies

Honey, 58

Honey bees, **Plate XIV**, 56–60

   activities, 56

   cultivation, 59

   pheromones, 56–57

   pollination, 58

   swarms, 58

   wax, 58

Honeydew, 2, 63

Horse flies, 61–62

House dust, 32

House flies, 94, 96

Hover flies, **Plate XVI**, 63–67

   cultivation, 64

   defense mechanism, 65

   pollination, 63, 65

   sound, 65

Hydrogen peroxide, 58

I

Inchworms, 19

Insect art, 102

Insect attractants

   automobile exhaust, 74

   formaldehyde, 74

   heptaldehyde, 74

   light flashes, 49, 51

   UV light, 74

Insect collecting, 99–100

Insect mounting, 99–100

Insect poisons

   acetone, 46

   ethyl acetate, 99

   malathion, 81

Insect predators

   antlions, 6

   crane flies, 38

   dragonflies, 43, 47

   hover flies larvae, 64

   lacewings, 71

   midges, 9

   mole crickets, 80

   syrphus flies, 66

   wasps, 66–67

Insect splats, **Plates I–XXIV**

   definition, ix

Invertase, 58

J

Jumping plant lice, **Plate XVII**,
   68–70

K

Kettle, D.S., 9

L

Lacewings, **Plate XVIII**, 71-72
  camouflage, 71
  defense mechanism, 16
Leptoconops. See Midges
Libellulidae. See Skimmers
Lice
  jumping plant, **Plate XVII**,
    68-70
Linnaeus, Carolus, xvii
Lip-trap, 63
Locust
  desert, 53
  sound, 53-54
  swarms, 53-54
Lovebugs, **Plate XIX**, 73-76
  damage to automobiles, 74
  defense mechanism, 75
Luciferin, 49
Lydia deshaisiana, 21

M

Maggots, 64, 94
Malaria, 86, 90
Malathion, 81
Mandibles, 4
Mansonia. See Mosquitoes,
  mansonia
Measuring worms, 19
Melanoplus differentialis. See
  Grasshoppers, American

Metamorphosis, 15-16
Mexican jumping bean, 21
Midges, **Plate XX**, 77-78
  biting, **Plate III**
Mole crickets, **Plate XXI**, 79-82
  control of, 81
  northern, 79
  short-winged, 79
  sound, 80-81
  southern, 79
  tawny, 79
Monarch butterfly, 23
  caterpillar, 16
Mosquitoes, **Plate XXII**, 83-93
  Asian tiger, 86, 91
  control of, 86
  cultivation, 87
  diseases carried by, 86, 89-90
  glades, 92
  larvae, 85
  malaria, 90
  mansonia, 93
  northern house, 89
  recognizing female, 84
  repellants, 86
  salt-marsh, 91
  sound, 84
  southern house, 89
  yellow fever, 88
Moths, **Plate V**, 14-24
  attraction to light, 14-15
  defense mechanism, 16

Stratiomyidae. *See* Soldier flies

Stylet, 68

Sugarberry (tree), 68

Swallowtail caterpillar, 16

Syrphidae. *See* Hover flies

Syrphus. *See* Syrphus flies

Syrphus flies, 66

    defense mechanism, 66

    sound, 66

T

Tabanus. *See* Horse flies

Tabanus americanus. *See* Horse
    flies

Tansey, 86

Taxonomy, xvii

    mnemonic, xvii

Tibicen canicurlaris. *See* Dog-
    day cicadas

Tibicen resh. *See* Southwestern
    cicada

Tibicen resonans. *See* Cicadas

Tiger swallowtail butterfly,
    Plate V

    camouflage, 22

    caterpillars, 22

Tipula spp. *See* Crane Flies

Tipulidae. *See* Crane flies

Torticidae. *See* Tortricid moths

Trichoptera. *See* Caddisflies

U

UV light, attractant, 74

V

Viceroy butterfly, 24

Volucella. *See* Volucella flies

Volucella flies, 66

W

Wasp (game), 101

Western tiger swallowtail, 22

Worms

    canker, 20

    corn earworm, 20

    corn rootworm, 40

    inch, 19

    measuring, 19

    sod, 21

    spruce budworm, 21

Y

Yellow fever, 86, 89, 92

Z

Zygoptera. *See* Damselflies

FIELD NOTES

FIELD NOTES

.

SPLAT SKETCHES

About the Author

Mark Hostetler was born (1965) in Nigeria (Africa)—where his parents were teachers at a university in Nsukka, but was raised in Columbus, Indiana (a small, illustrious town situated smack-dab in the middle of the corn belt). He spent his youth attempting to tip over sleeping cows in pastures (an ever popular Midwestern myth), catching flies and feeding them to his pet toads, and dreaming about becoming a biologist who could help Marlin Perkins (of Wild Kingdom) film all those animals. In his youth, he and his brother also ran an auto-detailing business that involved washing insect parts off the surfaces of sport cars (destiny? . . . hmmmm).

Mark has just finished his Ph.D. in the Department of Zoology, University of Florida. While dreaming about unique ways to teach science to the public, he is also conducting research. His research consists of attempting to determine why different species of birds utilize different suburban landscapes around North America. Mark is also focusing much of his efforts on educating and convincing private property owners and developers to design their landscape to attract local wildlife by planting native vegetation. His ultimate goal is to drastically reduce the number of lawns (i.e., turf) that exist in North America.

OH MY! MORE INSECTS AND RODENTS AND BIRDS ... FROM TEN SPEED PRESS:

DEAD SNAILS LEAVE NO TRAILS

**Natural Pest Control for Home and Garden
by Loren Nancarrow and Janet Taylor**

Simple and effective natural pest-control methods for chemical-free gardening, including beneficial plants, eliminating ants, roaches, and rodents indoors and out, nontoxic flea relief for pets, and much more.   160 pages

FURTIVE FAUNA

**A Field Guide to the Creatures Who Live on You
by Roger Knutson**

Take a closer look at such fascinating little fellows as the eyebrow mite and the tooth amoeba, not to mention the dreaded tropical chigoe which can lay thousands of eggs in places you'd rather not think about. Fully illustrated, this book gives a whole new meaning to the term "a perfect host."   96 pages

THE COMPLEAT COCKROACH

**A Comprehensive Guide to the Most Despised
(and Least Understood) Creature on Earth
by David Gordon**

This exhaustive and irreverent look at the lowly cockroach showcases its history, habits, and cultural significance. Lavishly illustrated, this is a fun, fact-filled tribute to one of nature's most enduring triumphs (350 million years old and able to withstand a nuclear blast).   192 pages

WHAT BIRD DID THAT?

**A Driver's Guide to Some
Common Birds of North America
by Peter Hansard and Burton Silver**

The first scholarly treatment of ornithological dejecta, or bird droppings. Over 45 detailed entries depict typical bird "splays," and describe each bird's habitat and food.   64 pages